ENDORSE[

"I value a book only if I recognize the truth of it. It has added value if I recognize names and places that are familiar to me. This is what happened to me when I read my friend's book on New Guinea where, exactly fifty years ago, I had served in the army.

Recently, I re-visited the island and was surrounded by hundreds of Papuans, still living in the stone age outwardly, but now with radiant faces, singing hymns to Jesus and ever so eager to hear more about Him.

The work of Jacques and his team-mates has borne much fruit. This book tells you about how and why they did it."

—Brother Andrew,
Open Doors International

"This personal account of God's miraculous intervention is a wonderful affirmation of the liberating and life transforming power of the gospel. A valley of darkness, fear and oppression is transformed into a land of hope, love and spiritual light. The blind received sight, the lame walked, the deaf heard, the dead raised to life and the good news preached to the poor. God is still in the same "business," whether to a stone age people darkened by tradition and self destruction or to a fiber-optic community of people blinded and crippled by invention and self achievement. This is a glorious testimony to the Son of God who sets men and women free."

—Rev. Chris Thomas,
International Director of Torchbearers

THE SECRET OF NABELAN KABELAN

FROM WARRIORS TO BROTHERS

JACQUES H. TEEUWEN

WALKING TOGETHER PRESS
ESTES PARK · JENTA MANGORO

© 2024 Walking Together Press

Published in 2024 by
Walking Together Press
Estes Park, Colorado USA
Jenta Mangoro, Jos, Plateau Nigeria
walkingtogether.press

ISBN: 978-1-961568-72-3

The Secret of Nabelan Kabelan
Portions translated from *Das Geheimnis von Nabelan Kabelan,* 1997 CLV, by permission
Revised and updated

Cover design by D. Thaine Norris
Typeset in Adobe Garamond Pro by D. Thaine Norris

CONTENTS

Publisher's Foreword ix
Introduction xi
Preface xv
Remembrances of a Child 1
War Comes to the Netherlands 9
In Poland 15
The Collapse 25
From the Depth 47
The Occupation 61
Departure for Irian Jaya 77
Into the Stone Age 89
The Land Forgotten by God 93
Dirty Noses and Dirty Needles 95
A Gift for Priscilla 99
Fear 101
Nabelan Kabelan 105

Flames of Love	111
Old Passions	117
Perilous Proclamation	119
Chocolate And Mbawy	123
New Names, New Hairstyles	129
The Big Plunge	133
Steadfast Continuance	143
Snatched from Destruction	147
"I Am the Dead Man"	153
Everything in Common	157
From Savage to Student	161
No Bibles, Please!	165
Missing, Believed Killed	169
Mburumburu Goes Home	179
End of an Era	183
Conversation with Jacques and Ruth Teeuwen	187

Teeuwen Family: John Mark, Priscilla, Andrew, Jacques, Stephen, Ruth

PUBLISHER'S FOREWORD

Jacques teeuwen's *The Secret of Nabelan Kabelan* has been published for decades in various forms and in several languages: Dutch, German, Hungarian, and Polish. However, only a short, self-published booklet has ever been available in English, and it contains only the family's missionary experiences in Irian Jaya.

This new edition, published by Walking Together Press with assistance and contributions from the Teeuwen family, is based on the 1997 German book *Das Geheimnis von Nabelan Kabelan* published by CLV, which has granted permission for the translation and subsequent English publication. Additional Irian Jaya stories that were unique to the English booklet have been added to this edition.

Special thanks goes to H. Ebehard Roell, with assistance from his wife Debbie, for the translation work.

Note that the author uses "Irian Jaya" as the country name for his stories of missionary service amongst the Dani people. Today the region is known as "West New Guinea."

INTRODUCTION

"Based on my childhood and teenage years, probably no one would have assumed that one day I would serve the Lord Jesus Christ in the jungles of Irian Jaya," said Jacques Teeuwen, because "religion was as far removed from my practical life as Irian Jaya itself." This book therefore also includes the author's "backstory."

As a twelve-year-old, Jacques experienced the occupation of his country by the Germans. He explains how the pernicious ideology of National Socialism was initially received with enthusiasm by many, and that he himself fell for the deception. However, one disappointment after another followed, until at last hunger, fleeing, and the death of his companions forced him to change his mind. Then a profound change occurred in Jacques that led to a chapter of life as different from the wartime chapter as day is from night.

His story leads us into the strange world of Irian Jaya, the western half of the island of New Guinea, north of Australia and just south of the equator. With a length of 813 miles and a width of 375 miles, New Guinea is the second largest island in the world. It is home to the Bird of Paradise and many other types of rare animals and plants and has rugged mountains rich with mineral resources. Since 1962 the western area has belonged to Indonesia, while the eastern part of the island, Papua New Guinea, is an independent state.

Irian Jaya is a country one can hardly imagine to be more contradictory, with the most varied climate and areas of vegetation. In coastal areas it is tropically hot and, especially in the south, largely covered with swamps. Rainforests are widespread and reach a height of up to 1,200 meters (about 4,000 ft). Other parts of Irian Jaya have a mountainous climate and even regions of eternal snow. If you swim in the warm tropical ocean in the south, at the same time you can see the snow-covered mountains.

The entire length of the island is crossed by several mountain ridges—some with gold-bearing rock formations—which in the west run into mountains and hill country. The highest peak in Irian Jaya is the Puncak Jaya with a height of 5,030 meters, over three miles, higher than all the peaks of the Alps. The mountains are rough and steep, and countless waterfalls plunge into the valleys. Clouds form rapidly and almost daily heavy thunderstorms develop. Not until one knows about the inaccessibility of the inner mountain regions can one understand why many of the tribes living there did not encounter people from the outside world until the 1960s. They simply lived in the Stone Age.

It was one of these tribes, the Dani, that Jacques Teeuwen and his wife Ruth joined. Their mission station was in the Central Highlands, where the villages are at 1,500 meters and higher. The climate here is not as much determined by the time of year, but rather by remarkable daytime temperature fluctuations; hot during the day and bitterly cold at night. Since the huts of the Dani provided little protection against the nightly cold, sickness was a common experience.

At the time of the Teeuwen's story, the Dani had a population of about 100,000 people. Their language was but one of the estimated 300-plus in New Guinea. The Dani have only twenty-two letters in their alphabet, and some of these have no equivalent in our alphabet. For "red" and "white" they have only one word, and for the future they have various forms, which are unknown in our language. Everything that goes beyond one month is considered a distant reality and is deemed uncertain.

In the last twenty years much has changed in Irian Jaya. Civilization has found an entrance with all its negative consequences. Rainforests have been cut down, mineral resources exploited and roads built. The Indonesian government forced the mountain tribes to move, and now they live in social poverty and only perform their traditional rites for tourists. In recent years several books have been published that are critical of these developments and give serious thought to the mission.[1]

Precisely for that reason Jacques Teeuwen's book is so interesting, because he and his family came to a tribal culture that was basically untouched, something that is practically nonexistent today. Never did he encourage the indigenous people to abandon their traditional way of life. Major cultural changes did happen, but always at the initiative of the tribesmen themselves.

Twenty years have passed since the author first published his experiences. The book has already been published in several languages, but now the possibility for a German edition has arisen. In 1993 I began with my American friend Bernardine Heckman to translate the English manuscript into German. At this point I want to thank all my friends who have encouraged me in this work; also, my husband, Manfred, and my brother Karl for their worthwhile help.

In an appendix, I have the notes of an interview I had with the Teeuwens.

Micheldorf, Oberoesterreich, Summer, 1997
Dr. phil. Veronika Trautmann

---

1 Z. B. Mathieu Debout: *Kinder der Steinzeit? Papua zwischen Militär und Mission im Hochland West-Neuguineas.* Moers, Edition Aragon, 1991.

PREFACE

"**W**HY HAVE you not written a book about your experiences in Irian Jaya?"

It was 1977 when Johnny Mitchell first posed this question. At that time Johnny was the vice president of an American mission for which I held a series of lectures.

"Nobody ever asked me about that," was my reply.

"Well, then I am the first one to ask that question!" Johnny was always straight forward.

At that time I did not think much about it, but Johnny's question remained with me. I put a fleece before the Lord: the next time I go to the United States and someone mentions that book to me, I will see that as a sign to start one.

After a while I conducted a series of lectures for a whole month in the eastern part of the States, however no one ever brought up the subject.

On the 13th of November 1977, Wilbert and Nellie Bakker took me to the airport right after the Sunday service. At that time, they belonged to Grace Church in Ridgewood, New Jersey[1] and had been hospitable to me on an earlier visit to Florida. The airport building was already in

---

1 This church supported the Teeuwens financially during their stay in West New Guinea.

view when Nellie suddenly asked, "Yesterday six of us were at your lecture. We agreed that you should put your experiences on paper. Why have you not authored a book?"

"I will write it!" I shouted. My voice was much louder than the small room in the car would have required.

Since then, dozens of people in various countries have brought up the subject. "You should write a book." In response I was able to respond that I a completed manuscript in my drawer!

I frequently met people who had heard my reports and expressed interest in my book, but I never found a publisher. However, I have not gone out of my way to find one either, since our people are inundated with literature of all kinds. After all, there are so many other important subjects.

Twenty years have passed, but now it is time. The narrative that follows is not meant to be an autobiography, although it contains a lot of firsthand experiences. Neither was it supposed to be just a story of the missionary work in Irian Jaya, nor a story of the development of Christian churches; too early for that! It is much more my desire to once again call to memory the things that God did in my life and in the people with which He surrounded me.

When the first burning of weapons took place, I was not yet in Irian Jaya, but I include this event because it is particularly important to the understanding of what follows. I keep the focus on Frank Clarke as a witness, among others, when the work of the Holy Spirit became visible early on.

Perhaps you will ask yourself if the things you will read are really true. For that I want to tell the following story:

A key figure in the revival on the island of Timor (southwest of Irian Jaya) once visited me at home. I had just received an edition of a well-known Christian magazine. It contained an article about the happenings in Timor, with the author of the article confessing that he could simply not believe the report.

I read this article to my guest. But he did not in the least allow any doubt. "How can one doubt that these things are impossible," he stated in a friendly way. "I experienced them myself."

In the same way, I take full responsibility that the experiences that follow in this book are true.

"He lifted me out of the slimy pit, out of the mud and mire; he set my feet on a rock and gave me a firm place to stand." (Psalm 40:2)

To the Lord be glory and honor.
Jacques Teeuwen

THE SECRET OF NABELAN KABELAN

REMEMBRANCES OF A CHILD

THE NETHERLANDS is a fascinating country. Every Dutchman whose heart is in the right place feels that way, even when he will never admit it. It is not in the character of Dutchmen to show their feelings—not even for a moment.

If a stranger would praise his home country with lots of words, the Dutchman would contemptuously shrug his shoulders and say in a derogatory way: "The Netherlands? Een kikkerland."[1]

But if an outsider attacked the so-called "Country of Frogs," then the Dutchman would become enraged like a lion whose young ones were stolen. He would scratch and kick, snort and bite out of anger, until he had recaptured what is rightfully his. That is possibly the reason so many coat-of-arms show a lion.

There was a time in history when, for eighty years, the Dutch defended their freedom with all their might. Enemies regularly surrounded the Netherlands. But one of them was particularly victorious—or was it simply an unreliable friend? The Netherlands is often called "the country of water," and the water counts as both friend and enemy. Every Dutch child is intuitively aware what, with much effort, he must memorize in primary school:

---

1 A frog country

Take away the Dutch farmer's guilders,
his pennies, and all his money;
if he only has his fertile soil,
he will disregard everything and whistle to himself.

And if you take away his fertile soil,
he will still keep the water
and pump it with his mill
until it runs dry—sooner or later.

But if you take away the water,
the lakes, the canals and the marshland,
then Holland has ceased to be Holland,
even if it can still be seen on the map.

The dunes will then become wilderness
and all the meadows will dry out.
There would be nothing left of my beautiful Holland,
because it cannot bear thirst.

Without this "Friend Water" the Netherlands cannot exist. And when this friend, in an unpredictable temper, suddenly becomes their enemy, then all Dutchmen know how to deal with it. When the stormy waves of the North Sea are whipped up and driven on by their racing ally, the wind, and lash the Netherlands' cheerful coasts and immovable dikes, then the battle is announced. The church bells ring in alarm to drive back every little drop and every angry wave. "Retreat! Retreat! The Dutchmen are coming." Sometimes the victories of the foaming water are transformed into a humiliating loss. Armed with shovels and sandbags, munitions boxes and cranes, here comes the counterattack.

However the strongest weapon of the Dutchmen is an unbelievable sense of humor, which under difficult circumstances rises to its greatest advantage.

When the wind finally dies down and the thunderstorm is over, the devastated dunes are again built up and the destroyed dikes are repaired.

"Nederland zal herrijzen" ("The Netherlands shall rise again") is not just an empty slogan!

The Dutch cannot afford to be unforgiving, since they need wind and water. When the waves peacefully, as if for reconciliation, wash up little white crests, everything is forgotten. Wind drives the sails of the windmills, and the aroma of millions of flowers blows over the dreamy countryside, where peaceful cows graze and farmers in wooden clogs do their jobs. Who can deny that the Netherlands is unique?

Among the nicest cities in the Netherlands, Haarlem takes one of the premier spots. This settlement on the Spaarne was declared a city as early as 1245. The saying "you can't hide your age" certainly doesn't apply. After over 700 years, Haarlem still retains a feeling of youthfulness, while the historic buildings of the city still convey a special sense of dignity. Possibly the layout of the famous market contributes to the youthful and carefree aspect. Only a playful disposition could have the idea of putting the meat market next door to the imposing cathedral St. Bavo, which has an internationally known organ with at least 500 pipes and seventy stops. This meat market, which was built later, is so attractive in its form and colors that disrespectful Dutch have expressed their assumption that the architect possibly drank too much of the local gin. The fine appearance of the "Bloemenstad" Haarlem can be explained by the well-known tulip fields, which can easily be reached from the city with a bicycle. In the spring the city center is amazingly beautiful. One is overcome by the captivating beds of daffodils, violet, white, and red hyacinths, as well as extravagant masses of spring flowers in all colors. It is not surprising that a silver tulip is the most desired prize of the annual organ celebration in St. Bavo.

On March 30, 1928, a member of the registry in Haarlem dutifully recorded the following:

> "Jacques Hubert Teeuwen was born, son of Jacobus Hubertus Teeuwen and of Carolina Hol, married."

After paying a small administrative fee, my parents received the required certificate. My entry into this world—should somebody doubt it—was confirmed by high authority. Four daughters of the Teeuwens had already seen the light of the world ahead of me. About ten years later, two boys were added.

Father and mother Teeuwen both came from large families and knew how they had to control that crowd of children. They were committed to give their kids the best despite tough times, yet their father's meager income as a police officer set clear limits. My father came from the southern part of the Netherlands and was Roman-Catholic until he met my mother. At that time there was no intermarriage between denominations. That is why my father left the church and became a Protestant, like my mother. As a result, because of the "lost son," the relationship within the family became fractured. Nobody talked with each other for several years. In my parents' house it was customary to read short portions of the Bible after the main meal. If one could repeat the last words read, then that was sufficient proof that one had understood everything. Afterwards everyone should pray quietly. Only the youngest ones said a short prayer aloud.

The services in our church were terribly boring and seemed to go on forever. During the approximately two-hour ceremony I got more jabs into my ribs from my parents than during the rest of the week at home. What good was it that a large clock was mounted on the back wall? Every two or three minutes I turned around furtively to avoid additional smacks, but the result was frustrating. Most often it appeared that the hands on the clock in the intervening period hadn't moved at all. Apart from that, the people in the row behind us stared at me for my improper behavior. Their looks were piercing, as though they wanted to send me to torturous pain in hell.

The only bright spot was found in two peppermint candies, which belonged to the service as much as the black jackets and pinstriped pants of the pastor and the deacons. At home we had the habit of cutting the peppermint candy into four equal parts to be able to suck the only source of our comfort as long as we could.

I don't want to put the responsibility on the pastor alone. Nevertheless, I do arrive at the sad reality that I cannot remember ever having heard something from the podium that was fascinating, interesting, or challenging. It was a relief for me when political developments brought an end to my church attendance, from which I profited so little. They found their end when I was twelve years old.

School was also not exactly fun. Long before that fateful day on which I entered the first class, the thought gave me stomach cramps. One of my few buddies looked forward to school, which I simply could not understand. I was nervous because of the many kids. Besides, I had to walk around ten minutes to get there, and I was never alone that far from home. My parents wanted to walk with me only on the first day. After all, I was now a "big boy."

Contrary to all hope, the fearsome first day of school finally arrived. Encouraged by my older sisters, who already had a few years' experience with going to school, we ended our breakfast somewhat happily. Led by the hand of my mother, who smiled and said encouraging words, it seemed to work. I even had some hope that I would survive everything. But when we entered the building it was all gone. The students of the higher classes were much bigger and wilder than I had imagined. They looked down at us little ones with contempt and simply ignored us. One heard the voice of the director, which boomed happily over the noise, giving instructions and greeting the older students after their summer vacation. But the worst thing was the depressing smell of carbolic acid. I already felt nauseous and had to retch a little when the first-grade teacher saw me. She addressed me kindly and stooped down to welcome me into her class. But a unique smell emanated from her; also which I did not know from home. On a birthmark from her chin grew three tiny hairs that somehow got too close to me.

For me there was only one way in which I could escape that awkward and threatening situation. I started to cry, and not only a little or subdued, but with full volume, with which my pent-up fear disappeared. My uncontrolled sobbing created no small disturbance in a class where approximately forty young and mostly trembling newcomers to the world tried desperately to prove that they had suddenly become big boys and girls. Not a chance! The boy who sat next to me was the first to start to cry likewise. The teacher suggested that my mother should leave the class, but that didn't help.

They called my sister out of the second class to try to comfort me. One year earlier she had been put into the school without even crying one tear.

Confidently she entered the classroom. A few minutes later she left—crying. Meanwhile, I continued to bawl. Next, my sister from the sixth class was called to encourage me. She, too, left the classroom with a handkerchief pressed closely to the face.

"I want to go home," I sobbed in response to the teacher trying to show more self-assertion. Full of frustration she played her final trump card: "Fransje!" Little Fransje was an advanced pupil. Self-assured he had entered the classroom, and with a casual but friendly hand motion, dismissed his mother and aunt, who had accompanied him on his first school day. His fancy silk suit and the matching tie were probably purchased for this special occasion. Fransje was full of confidence; he could manage this situation. He marched to the table, which was meant for him, sat down, kept his back straight and crossed his arms across his chest—just as it was expected of him. If there was someone who possessed self-control and could pass on some of his confidence, then that was Fransje. That was why he was put next to me. There really was something in his behavior that impressed me, but it was not sufficient to stop my crying. When through my tears I risked a glance at Fransje, I noticed that his lower lip twitched. A thick tear rolled slowly over his pink cheek and landed on his flawless silk jacket.

I do not remember how, but eventually we ended up in a ceasefire. It was a compromise: If they allow me to leave at twelve o'clock and I could return to my parents, then I would stop crying.

In time I got accustomed to the school, but I never really had any fun there, but I did enjoy participating in games in the schoolyard. Many times the whole of my class bent over laughing when I purposefully made one of my dumb remarks. On the outside I was one of them, but under the surface I felt uncomfortable. With one simple exception I never felt that a teacher had an interest in me or liked me. Since most of my experiences in school were negative, I didn't think it was serious when the experiences of the Second World War put an end to my education in the eighth grade.

Although I was born in a city, I was never a city boy because I loved nature above everything. The early morning hours held a special fascination for me. In grade school I would often be the first in the schoolyard. In the quiet of the morning, I would hear the chirping of the sparrows, which until then still had the schoolyard to themselves. They were loud and rascally, just like the kids who would come later and release some steam before they entered the classroom.

Also, at home I was often the first one up. After a walk through the pantry, I would jump on my bicycle. Forest and dunes were not far away. The early morning hours have their own pull and awaken the senses in a special way. It was fun to listen to the humming of the wheels when they ran over the moist ground. Sparkling dewdrops drew a pattern of fragile beauty on the spiderwebs and flowers. Even rusted barbed wire could be a feast for the eyes. When the cold morning air finally had to give way, and the sun with its golden beams spread out like a magical fan across the land, then it was wonderful to be there. After the cool beginning it was nice to greet the sun and allow it to warm you.

But nothing fascinated me more than water. There was nothing more secretive when at sunrise it lay there quietly like a silver mirror. What lay hidden directly under the still surface? Suddenly a nearly unnoticeable shiver ran through the reeds, which looked at themselves in the water, and mysteriously one waited to see what else would happen. At some distance one could barely hear what appeared like a coot come up out of the water. Ever increasing circles built around its gleaming body that had seemingly come out of nothing and now swam quietly around.

There was another way one could discover the secrets of the water—fishing, which likewise belonged to my childhood. A bamboo fishing rod equipped with a thin string and a sharp hook were ubiquitous in the countryside. For hours I sat patiently and observed the lure as it gently moved up and down. Even though often nothing happened, there was the expectation. The only disappointment was when the truly big fish either swam away or were caught by someone else. Irresistibly I was drawn to the water, where I spent the greatest part of my vacation.

WAR COMES TO THE NETHERLANDS

O**N MAY** 10th, 1940, the Second World War reached the Netherlands. On that tragic day I rose earlier than normal. There was something in the air that I could not explain. I got dressed and went downstairs. Much to my surprise my parents were already awake and fully dressed. They stood by the window and fixated on something in the sky. The radio was turned on, and I recognized the voice of the announcer. This was not the normal time of day to hear the news.

"Warnings of paratroopers," one could hear repeatedly. "Rotterdam, Strijen, Den Haag: Warnings of paratroopers . . ."

"I think they must have military exercises," my mother said several times. But by her facial expressions one could recognize that she herself didn't really believe it. We heard above us the threatening sound of droning plane engines and could already recognize one plane. Suddenly small balls of black smoke rose around the enemy plane that seemed to have difficulty moving forward. Minutes later the agitated barking of exploding bombs caused the windows to rattle. We jerked every time we heard these sounds, as we were not used to such things. Harmless looking little black clouds remained until the wind drove them off. The bombs seemed disappointed; disappointed because they failed to achieve their purpose.

A few days later we saw a bomb make a perfect hit. Suddenly the high-flying bomber emitted a thick cloud of black smoke. Unexpectedly the plane changed course, executed a half circle and raced with increasing speed towards the ground. I wondered what would happen to the crew and instinctively my teeth began to chatter.

The army of the Netherlands was not able to withstand the well-trained and well-equipped Germans; besides, numerically they were far outnumbered. In one single attack, the German bombers reduced the whole center of Rotterdam to a heap of rubble. The German commander threatened that other cities would experience the same fate. After only five days of courageous resistance against the superior strength, the fear of the bombardments forced the Netherlands to submit. There was no other way out—the Netherlands were occupied. Subconsciously I assumed that life would never be the same.

From a twelve-year-old one cannot expect a whole lot of political insight. Since he barely has experience, he cannot yet evaluate developments and the complicated connections of higher politics he cannot grasp. He can only see the dealings of people from his own perspective and is unconscious of the goals and motivations of political leaders. Why should it have then been different with me? If at all, I could judge the happenings only by their exterior value.

Soon after the occupation of the Netherlands by the Germans, there were changes in our family. In place of whispers about the cruelty of the Germans, there were now heated discussions promoting National Socialism. It became clear that my father was enthusiastic about Hitler's new ideas, while my mother argued against them. But as time passed, she ended up on the wrong side. In case of an attack on the Netherlands, the Allied Powers promised help; but that did not happen. So what could one expect from the Allies?

In the first days of the occupation, rumors spread about the rough dealings of the Germans. But I had stood by the edge of the road when they marched in with smiling faces and distributed chocolate and cigarettes to the nervous population. If those were our enemies, who needed friends? The attitude of our Queen was also instructive and confusing.

Prior to the war she had assured her subjects that members of the Royal House of Orange would never flee. But shortly after the beginning of the fighting, the whole of the Netherlands' government had moved to foreign countries. When one looked at the events of the war, it was obvious that the Allies had lost their incentive for war, because the Germans were victorious all around—on land, in the ocean, and in the air. After the fiasco of Versailles in 1919, Hitler, as he claimed, saved his people from total destruction and provided freedom, work, and bread.

It was not surprising therefore that my father one day came through our door wearing the uniform of the Nazi Socialists and shortly after that worked for them full-time. That was reason enough for me to also attach myself to a youth organization since I also wanted to wear a uniform. In fact, I was given a uniform, but it didn't have gold stars and rather short sleeves. But that would change shortly.

After I got over some concerns I had at the beginning, I began to enjoy my participation. I met people who knew exactly what they wanted. Many of them had honorable ideals—smoking and drinking were scorned, and one didn't hear any dirty words. I enjoyed participating in the activities, and military exercises I considered especially exciting. We marched often through town to make people aware of us. In so doing, we beat the drums and let the flags fly, whereby the penetrating beat of the trumpets sounded like a call of victory. The rhythm of our stomping feet boomed across the old market, while we sang with all we were worth:

> "We are the youth,
> The future of our beloved country.
> We want to get to work
> And rebuild our great fatherland."

Sometimes people turned away, full of contempt. These individuals were confronted by our officials, and were forced to turn around and watch us, because it was considered high time that they would recognize the new political realities. Some of my school buddies envied me. On Saturday afternoons they sneaked out of the house to join us. When we marched through Haarlem, they followed us closely—unfortunate creatures, who were not allowed to wear our uniforms because their narrow-minded parents wouldn't allow it.

But there were also different reactions. Some of my comrades wouldn't talk to me anymore. When I met them on the street, they acted as if they didn't know me. Others turned away and spit in full disgust. For me it was only an expression of stupidity; something that one had to face temporarily for a good cause.

With Simon it was a different situation. We had been friends for a long time, rode our bicycles together, played soccer, and did our homework together. Additionally, I was drawn to him because Simon's uncle was the pastor of a church. As pastor, he allowed us to look for change which people had lost during the service. When we were lucky and found a coin, we hurried to a nearby pastry shop where we turned our find into huge numbers of biscuits.

When Simon's parents learned of my new membership, they told me in no uncertain terms that my way would lead me directly into hell, and that therefore I would be too dangerous a playmate for Simon. Further, they assured me that they would pray for me. From that day on Simon was like a stranger to me. It was as though an invisible curtain of silence, hate, and isolation fell in front of me.

Beginning on June 22, 1941, the war took on a new dimension due to the "Foresight of our great Leader." Adolf Hitler recognized the damaging intentions of the Soviet Union to march into Western Europe to kill our cultural heritage—that's how the German propaganda announced it. To escape this danger, victorious German troops penetrated Russia and beat into flight the so-called barbaric Slavic hordes. How reverently we sang our songs in which we praised the omnipotence which had sent us such a strong leader, who would save Europe. The belt buckle of the Germans carried the inscription, "God with us." Now we had become conscious of that meaning.

For the final victory it seemed only necessary to clean up the remaining opposition centers in the Russian steppe. The government urgently advertised for volunteers who would be prepared to enter the occupied countries. All those who wanted to help put an end to the communist threat to Europe once and for all were welcome in the "Thousand Year Reich"—this was the name given to the new empire that was to last for a thousand years.

Significant participation came from the Nazi movement in the Netherlands since it offered the opportunity to see something of the world at the same time. The adventure was enticing. Many young men wanted to take the chance for, after all, it is the Dutch tradition to support values and freedom. That's why young and old came in droves to the registration offices. Many of my buddies from the youth movement joined, and all committed themselves for the duration of the war. There was also the possibility to commit for two years, but that appeared too long to most, because who wanted to be in the military after the war?

For me it was an enormous setback that the State did not accept volunteers under eighteen years, and I would have to wait until 1946. By then, the war would surely be over and forgotten. It was deeply frustrating to be excluded for such an insignificant reason. What made me responsible for not being born earlier? Nevertheless, just like the others I felt like a fighter, who decidedly moved out to try his luck on the eastern front.

To bring a swift end to the war, the war machinery had to run. "Wheels must roll for the victory," was the slogan you could read everywhere. The soldiers needed food, and this had to be produced. Especially in the agrarian sector, workers were in short supply. Apart from that you must consider that the Russian army was thought to be broken. Never again did anyone want to give the Russians the opportunity to threaten Germany. To accomplish this in a friendly manner, large areas of Russia were occupied and remained under German supervision. Ukraine, the granary of Europe, needed workers. New settlements were to be built and one tried to win and train bold farmers. When I heard of these intentions I was fascinated, because that idea coincided with my love for nature. I always wanted to become a farmer like my grandfather, but in the Netherlands that was unlikely because of limited land and the large population. Although I wasn't sure if I could handle the continuous difficult work of the farmer, here was another consideration: we would be the supervisors and the cheap Russian workers would be our subjects. The condition to commit myself for two years to the Waffen SS seemed insignificant compared to the potential opportunities.

IN POLAND

In June 1943, a transport with volunteers left from the Netherlands heading towards eastern Europe, and I was among them. For four days our transport rolled eastward, where we envisioned a fantastic future. But first, we experienced long days on the train that barely moved forward, because regular air raids forced us to stop. At other times we were moved from the main circulation line to a different track, since the transport of the military and their materials had priority. "Wheels must roll for the victory." But nobody wanted to complain about the frequent stops. To be moving along counted, and we were part of the huge machinery of war. Together with millions of people we had found a goal—a life purpose. While the train moved forward mile after mile, like an unrolling carpet, our youthful, happy voices drowned out the rattle of the steam engine with the well-known song: "We want to march on, even when everything falls apart, for today Germany belongs to us, and tomorrow the whole world."

Then, when we had become hoarse from all the singing, we would sit together and start enthusiastic discussions about the better life that we wanted to lead.

To be able to effectively place us, we were divided in groups of ten and sent into various regions of Poland. Would we have our own rooms? Or who would be our roommates? Or would there be dormitories?

We chatted excitedly like children who had just been allowed to enter the colorfully decorated room full of Christmas presents.

When we reached our most exciting subject, we would reverently lower our voices. There were also a whole bunch of girls on the train, who were on their way to different camps. But they were probably determined to become wives of future "big farmers." These were fascinating thoughts for growing men, who only dared to talk to a girl in the presence of other boys. Generally we avoided all who wore skirts, as if we wanted to avoid an infection.

Above all, we were impressed by the perceptiveness of our capable leaders, for not even our parents had considered this delicate subject. If then our long-term plans concerning our future had already been so carefully considered, we could rest easy about the immediate future. Although we barely understood the words, we sang along to the soldiers' songs about the beauty of the female sex and fantastic fantasies. Meanwhile, the train drew ever closer to our destination.

Initially we thought that somebody was teasing us, but the group leader, himself a bit less certain, convinced us of the opposite—we had arrived at our destination. We dragged our suitcases through the loose sand. Nobody said a word when we stopped in front of a dilapidated schoolhouse. We were in one of the poorest regions of Poland. Our hope to be received with a warm meal evaporated like steam out of a teakettle.

The question of whether our beds had already been made or if we had to see to that ourselves seemed suddenly absurd because there were neither soups nor beds. There was absolutely nothing. We walked through the empty rooms until the full ridiculous picture dawned on us. After we had recovered from the initial shock, somebody started laughing—initially hesitatingly, but then louder and more boisterous, until even the pessimists were infected and joined in the laughter, which wiped away all the disappointment and tiredness. Against this challenge we wanted to stand strong, after all, we were pioneers and the future belonged to us. So, we got busy. We talked to a farmer in the area out of a few potatoes; from another we organized straw for sleeping. We borrowed a pot to cook our first potato meal. One craftsman and proud owner of a pocketknife began to carve a serving spoon as well as some unidentifiable tools that were supposed to be forks. As we were sitting on the floor we tried to stab the potatoes with our rustic tools and were enjoying ourselves.

As the sun set, we stretched ourselves out fully clothed, and finally experienced peace and rest. We were confident that things would get better.

But soon we realized that things would get much worse. We had spent several weeks in the camp and were totally independent; now we sought out farmers who would need our services. That's how I met Joseph. Early each morning, blue smoke rose from his property (which was about 300 meters from our camp) which had an alluring effect on me.

One could barely consider Joseph's house a farm. The stables were roughly hewn boards hammered together and covered with straw. There was no concrete floor; the cows sank up to their ankles in dirt and muck. These few bony and dirty creatures represented Joseph's riches and pride, while we looked at them with pity. A threshold between stable and courtyard was the only barrier between the dirt inside and outside of the stable.

The house was small and dirty, as well. Only he who was humble enough to bend down could enter through the front door. One couldn't tell when the yellow and black walls had last received a fresh coat of white paint.

Joseph was a friendly man. Although he was only in his early thirties, his hair was already thin. When the sun shone on his bare head, his good-natured attitude showed even more. He had a generous smile, through which it became obvious that he was missing several front teeth. When I asked him if he needed any help for his farmyard, he replied positively. His philosophy was as simple as his broken German: "You work well—I give you money. You don't work well—I don't give you money." When I agreed, he indicated that I should follow him, while he walked barefoot through the yard of sand and muck. As I carefully traipsed behind him, Joseph could barely hide his contempt, because I carefully, if unsuccessfully, attempted to keep my shoes clean.

Before handing me the hoe, Joseph showed me how to work the moss that served as a substitute for straw in the stables. Five minutes later I was all alone in the small forest.

At first the words "You work well—I give money" sounded like music to my ears. But soon I realized that it was quite hot in the forest. There were a lot of mosquitos, but no people to talk to. Also, I had underestimated the weight of the hoe. The heap of moss that I pulled from the forest floor was rather small.

When he came the next day to inspect my meager progress, his face expressed a mixture of amusement and amazement.

"It is what it is," he said, going back to an oft-used expression, fascinating in its simplicity. Nevertheless, he gave me some money. I was in high spirits until he explained that he needed more moss the next day. When I was busy hoeing the next morning, I asked myself if this was really what I wanted. It seemed to be a far cry from what it meant to be a "big farmer." And how could I in some way influence the war effort here? All possibilities seemed to be far away. Meanwhile the sun burned and the mosquitos stung mercilessly. Often—probably too often—I went to Joseph's humble abode to look at the clock and make sure I wasn't working overtime. That evening, I wasn't paid anything. "It is what it is," Joseph said with a shrug, letting me know that he wasn't interested in my returning the next day.

Then I was offered a "confidential" job. I sensed it was more like a punishment and not a promotion. In any case, I saw it as a warning to my comrades to not take anything lightly. But apparently, I did not have a choice. Together with a buddy who likewise had little success as a worker, I was assigned to another camp to make it habitable. Van Loon, a tall, blonde, strapping fellow, was a nice guy, friendly and loyal, but surely not among the smartest. He had problems expressing himself but made up for it by cursing.

The dilapidated school building where we were first housed seemed like a palace next to our new quarters. Here unbroken windows were a luxury. The paint on the walls was peeling; plaster had fallen from the ceiling and formed small piles on the floor, making it impossible to close the worn front door. The loft appeared to be the safest and coziest place to set up our quarters. When lying down, we could see the twinkling stars through damaged roof tiles.

Since there was no running water, we would wash ourselves the next morning in the water right next to the house, which probably served the ducks and geese earlier. Before we could wash our faces with the muddy water, we had to clear off the many water fleas with our cupped hands.

"Do you have a special request for your breakfast?" I asked Van Loon sarcastically. At noon our stomachs growled so much that we were forced to test our military skills by sneaking unnoticed into a neighboring potato field. Such actions resulted in the menu for the following days. It went so far that Van Loon didn't talk anymore about his stomach, but he simply called it his "potato cemetery." Occasionally, we also didn't mind blaming an innocent fox for the disappearance of a few chickens.

A few weeks later we met our former comrades and were moved to a different school. That place was a bit more comfortable than our previous quarters, namely bunk beds with straw mattresses. We were also given clothes, but they were not nearly sufficient for the approaching winter.

I was assigned to a country estate whose owner was in the military. The Polish caretaker laughed scornfully when he learned that I wanted to become a farmer. After he had watched my general clumsiness for a few days, he felt sorry for me. Perhaps he didn't want the other workers to be demoralized by my performance; at least he always found an easier job for me, away from the others. Perhaps he also protected me from the orders of the top boss for, after all, he was dealing with a member of the Arian race, whereas he was "only" a descendant of the Slavic race. We were constantly exposed to that propaganda such that we almost believed it ourselves. For us it was at least a welcome conviction, and whoever didn't want to believe it, had to learn it by force. The administrator had every reason to be careful. We were not even allowed to talk with the Russian and Polish "slaves." A comrade who had started to learn Polish was strongly corrected for that reason. This race discrimination along with German thoroughness, brought about many unpleasant situations. Once, when I worked on a small farm, the wife of the farmer experienced a major embarrassment. She had cooked for all the workers but wasn't sure about the order of seating. "Slaves" could not sit at the same table as the Dutchmen, who had been personally labeled by the leader a pearl in the crown of the German countries. But maybe this pearl was not as shiny as the Germans themselves? At any rate, in the end, three tables were set up: One for the Germans, one for me, and one for the "slaves."

It was only during the potato harvest that the organizer did not discriminate. A long row of potatoes was plowed up, and each worker was given an equally long portion to harvest, which had to be brought to a certain place. For me it was painful, for I had neither the dexterity or a system like the others. All were quickly done with their work and sat on the empty baskets, while the tractor plowed up the next row. I stood there, legs straddling the row and hanging my head, digging doggedly for the potatoes and stones. I had to be careful that the tractor didn't pass over me.

I wondered if more potatoes were hidden in my area. Whenever I thought that I had succeeded and could just relax for a moment on my basket, I heard the voice of the driver as he plowed. Already the stamping and snorting of the horses approached, their leather belts squeaked, the wheels crunched, and mercilessly the torture started over.

One day when I returned from work, Van Loon called to me: "Teeuwen, you are supposed to report to the organizer."

I had now been nearly a year in Poland, and overall, I didn't find it that bad. Among the volunteers in the camp a special feeling of unity had developed. Through military exercises, work, and years of privation, we were steeled in body as well as in souls. We were aware that we were on the way to becoming the kinds of men that would be needed on the frontlines (although our leader maintained the opposite). But overall, I had found the work in the country estate enjoyable.

When I was told to report, I reviewed the last few days in my head, wondering what could be the purpose of this summons. Had I done anything wrong? I had not skipped any lessons recently. We had worked out a somewhat failsafe system to create some interesting variety in our lives. A few days earlier we had informed our employer that we had to travel on "business," which didn't sound unreasonable when you consider that country estates in remote Russia should belong to us soon. The plan went awry only once when, during our "business trip," our organizer decided to visit several farms where we were expected to be. It was difficult to not let his supervisors know that we were not where we were supposed to be. The awkwardness of the situation angered him more than our absence. I considered all these things before I was called to his office.

"You have been picked to be trained as an officer in our movement," I was informed. The camp director obviously enjoyed the privilege of informing me and was happy for me. Since I was the only one in our camp to receive this offer, it was an honor. But it would mean further military training and further schooling. Our "business travel" exploits would cease and besides, I had to leave my buddies. For the most part, we had bonded with each other. We had experienced privation together and mastered it. And I would leave all that! A few weeks later, when I left the camp, it felt as though I was leaving home.

Somewhat worried, I got on the train that would take me into the mountains in the south. Apparently tough training awaited me there. I was no longer naive, but the stories I heard from others indicated that they had experienced much worse than I.

We would build an international troop and that meant certainly that there would be much competition. Would I be able to keep up, and would the others be good comrades?

When I arrived at the training center my doubts remained. More than a hundred men, some of whom already had a rank, participated in the schooling. Some were at least twice as old as I. When I was introduced to the officers, I was nervous. Most of them were SS officers; medals and stripes adorned their uniforms. Several had had amputations and limped; they had experienced the reality of war and knew how to teach beginners. One comfort for me was that I was not the only one who felt self-conscious. Most of the others felt the same, which could not be covered up by exaggerated voices and feigned indifference.

In the end it all turned out differently. Of course there were sport competitions, military exercises, and the use of light weapons, which was not child's play. The training was hard, though not unfair. It was not a matter of "natural selection" to remove those who were considered unsuited for military leadership positions. The main emphasis in the schooling was rather directed to ideology, and that was constantly emphasized.

Fate had determined that our race would play an extraordinary role in history. We were the lords. The whole world belonged to us, and every obstacle had to retreat. But did we have the courage to walk in the footsteps of those who had given their lives on the battlefield? Were we ready to deal with the "reactionaries," who were creating chaos in their home countries?

One group of these reactionaries, of which it was claimed that they were continually working for confusion, were believing Christians. It was said that they believed long-abandoned ideas and didn't want to submit. For such stubbornness there was only one method to force them to be quiet: wipe them out. One officer reported how he participated in the elimination of an unteachable pastor. Since some of us came from Christian families, the mood that morning was somber.

Shortly after my arrival in Poland I had decided that it was simply impossible for one being to rule the whole world. For that reason, I had abandoned the last religious practice I had until then: a murmured, memorized prayer at noon.

If one truly wanted to show responsibility and love for one's home, there was no other choice but to deny spirituality; so they said. After all, that is how we would become trusted leaders. We could shoulder the responsibility to protect our people and to free them, and we could prove ourselves worthy of the confidence of our leader.

We had possibly not recognized the full sense and the exclusiveness of what was expected from us. But when we thought about what was involved—to protect the civilized world from destruction—then we had no other choice. Committed volunteers had sacrificed their lives in the defense of these values. Therefore, we, too, wanted to do whatever was necessary in blind obedience. With renewed determination we started singing the song of soldiers: "Leader, order, we follow you."

After two months, with the training nearing the end, my initial hesitation was removed, and I began to feel well. A recruiter came to our training camp with the opportunity to extend our commitment, which only cowards refused. I had succeeded, was promoted, and carried the black stripes of officer candidate. The sports medal on my left breast pocket could have been a bit larger. But most important were the red-covered shoulder pieces (with the words "war volunteer") which I carried proudly: that meant that I was a volunteer for the Waffen SS. Now I only needed to wait for my seventeenth birthday to enter the active service—in other words another nine months. At least I was on the right path.

It became apparent that there was not much time left to wear my stripes and badges. The opportunity to exchange them for silver or gold never came. Once I had the shoulder boards, they were no longer so important to me. But they did move me up a level and I became assistant to the camp commander, who had eighteen young men under his command. Everything that wasn't related to administration was now my responsibility. I didn't belong anymore to the friendship circle; now the others were obliged to salute me. But that was only fun in the beginning. Inwardly, I despised the troops under me. Most of them were younger than I and had not received nearly as thorough training. Secretly, I considered them to be wimps and I struggled to teach them military drills. On the farm where I helped, my military rank—however low it might be—also gave me a special position. The others saw this as something of a threat, and I was still too naive to understand why. The "good old days" on which we gathered potatoes or went on "business trips" seemed to be over.

THE COLLAPSE

MEANWHILE, OUR attention was taken up by other, more important things. The reports from the front were no longer as enthusiastic and victorious as they had been at the beginning. Of course, no one with any sense harbored the slightest doubt about our victory, because our leader had everything under control. He had promised us when we pledged our loyalty and unconditional obedience. "Fuehrer, command! We will follow you," was still our motto. But we couldn't completely ignore the daily news, either. In Russia, the country of our future, one city after another was evacuated. Ukraine, the breadbasket of Europe, which was to become our home, had fallen back into the hands of the Bolsheviks. According to official reports, it was a general and strategic shortening of the frontlines. It seemed no longer necessary to maintain the occupation of those vast areas of scorched earth called Russia. The plan for the coming spring was to recapture those desolate lands in connection with our final assault.

In January, 1945, I was supposed to take an agricultural exam in the town of Elbing (now in Poland), which was not far from our camp. I set off one morning, but I never arrived because there were no more trains to Elbing, as the town was in the firing range of the Russian artillery. I was glad I could return to our camp, where I reported to our leader. We agreed that the situation was serious. Suddenly the possibility of being overrun by the Russians had become a reality. Probably one could not assume that the Russians would be friendly to people who had fought against them.

The local party leader, however, issued a completely different order: No one was allowed to leave the area without his express permission. The order was: "Resist to the last man." But how were we supposed to defend ourselves, as there were no military units stationed in our area, and we had no weapons? If the official strategic line was "retreat and reorganize," why couldn't we apply this to our situation? So, we secretly worked out plans for our retreat. We had to inform our troops and pack food and clothes. Everyone was allowed to take a small suitcase with personal belongings. The German owner of a nearby farm, who had similar plans, provided us with a wagon and two horses. As soon as it got dark, we began to load the wagon. A little later we set off and left our camp in complete silence. Although we had put on all the clothes we could wear, we were still bitterly cold. An icy east wind blew through every layer of our clothing. For hours we trudged over snow-covered surfaces through the bleak night. At one point we stopped to have a bite to eat, but our bread was frozen like rock. The coffee I was carrying under my coat in my canteen was a block of ice. During the short break, the soles of my shoes also froze to a stiff mass, making every step more difficult. Now it was no longer necessary to tell everyone to be quiet, for all were too tired to talk. But nobody complained or suggested we look for a place to stay for the night, because the distant roar of the Russian artillery kept us moving.

Long after midnight, we stumbled into a deserted youth hostel. We didn't bother to take off our clothes and fell onto our beds. A little later we were told that we could get a warm meal, but nobody got up for it.

Like an explosive projectile, the camp leader's shrill whistle woke us up the next morning after a dreamless night. Dazed and sleepy faced, the tired youngsters began to stir. Standing up, we downed a cup of hot coffee. The horses were harnessed to the wagon again. "Szybko, szybko," urged a voice, forgetting that we didn't speak any Polish. "Hurry up, hurry up." The horses shook their heads as if to protest the poor working conditions and overtime. Then we were on the road again. It was still bitterly cold.

The wind blew with undiminished force, but at least it was no longer dark. We trudged through the snow, packed tightly together. Nobody said a word, not a single sarcastic joke was heard, not even the question of where we were going or how long this ordeal would last. We marched along in silence, just away from the war, away from the Russians.

Several hours later, a spectacle in front of us attracted our attention: a babble of voices, noise of vehicles, crunching snow. "We ran into the frontline, instead of moving away from it," was my first thought. When we came around a bend, I realized that my assumption had been wrong. But this realization did not make things any easier. My breath was taken away when I realized we had happened onto a main road which, to our great dismay, was packed with horse-drawn carriages and people, all heading west. Some army officers were shouting to clear the way for their cars, because they were driving towards the front. But nobody complied, because it was simply impossible to get through. Snow was packed next to the road, so there was no way to get around it. The vehicles of the people fleeing to the west were loaded with the most unimaginable things. Our luggage consisted mainly of oats for the horses and food for our own needs; there was also a live pig among them. But here, whole room furnishings, sewing machines and bedding were transported. The old, the sick and the children who could not walk, were enthroned on the dangerously loaded carts. You didn't have to be an expert to realize that many of these passengers wouldn't be able to last much longer. Obviously, some of them had already passed away as the cold and exhaustion had taken their toll. Next to the wagons, women and older children walked, whose husbands and fathers were at the front, fighting for a better future.

When we reached a small town that day, the chaos was overwhelming. The narrow streets were packed with carts, some of which had collapsed under the crushing weight. The horses became increasingly nervous and no longer responded to the commands of their drivers. Tense and agitated people were running around everywhere, trying to find a place to sleep, or a place to warm a meal. One woman was hysterically cursing Hitler, because now it didn't seem to matter anymore. A soldier had been hanged for stealing in the market square. He had disregarded the warning notices that had been posted all over town: "Looters and thieves will be executed." But nobody paid attention to the dangling body.

A woman was trying to make her way in the opposite direction. On the sled she was pulling was a small coffin. The woman was not crying, but her face was full of sorrow. A few days later, no one would bother to bury their dead because there were simply too many of them and the earth was frozen solid. While others struggled to find accommodation in overcrowded houses, we reported to the local Hitler Youth Headquarters. For us it was not a problem to find sleeping space, because they still needed young people to continue the war. Our "retreat for reorganization" sounded perfectly plausible. We were given enough space according to our wishes.

After a good night's sleep, we were called by our guide. In a subdued voice he informed us of his decision. For the moment we had escaped immediate danger, and there were trains here carrying refugees to West Germany. The leader saw his responsibility fulfilled and said that from now on everyone would be on their own. Within a few minutes nearly all the boys were on their way to the station. That was the last I saw most of them.

I was the only one who decided not to go to the station. "Why should I be in a hurry?" I asked myself calmly. The thought of the many jostling people and the panicked rush everywhere made me uncomfortable. The room at the headquarters was comfortable; why should I leave it? And where should I go? It didn't even occur to me that I could try to make it back to the Netherlands. A little later I strolled aimlessly through the city, feeling more like a spectator than a participant. But it was so cold, uncomfortable, and boring that by evening I had enough and made my way to the train station. There I looked at the long row of cattle cars which were crammed with people and their few possessions. People waited anxiously for the departure time. "When is the train due to leave?" I asked the crowd. "In a few hours at the earliest," came the reply. "Maybe I'll go with it, after all," I thought and went back to the headquarters to get my things.

When I returned to the station, the train was still there. With great difficulty I squeezed into one of the carriages. Once again, I asked when the approximate departure time was. "In a few hours at the earliest," someone replied in a monotone voice. I stood there, waiting and freezing. The people next to the door insisted that the door remained closed because of the cold. But the cold still spread, and the air became unbearably stuffy. After a few hours I'd had enough, because we hadn't made a single meter progress.

"Can I go outside, please?"

I wriggled my way through to the door and jumped out of the car. The crisp, cold air was invigorating. I was so convinced that the train wouldn't start moving that I left my suitcase in the carriage. I enjoyed a peaceful night's sleep at the headquarters. When I returned to the station the next morning, the train had gone—my suitcase with it!

The situation at the front became more manageable. The Russians had obviously adopted German strategies, which had proven to be successful. They didn't push forward as quickly as possible, but rather surrounded large areas, which they then cut off to destroy the enemy troops in so-called encirclement battles. We were inside one of these pockets. The front didn't come any closer but passed us and then cut us off. For us this meant a breather. An abandoned dairy was converted into a kitchen. For days I helped provide food to the stream of refugees that passed in large numbers. When the stream of refugees stopped, it didn't make sense for me to stay any longer. I boarded one of the last trains before the boilers were closed. This train was almost empty.

We made slow progress through the dull, wintry landscape. The steam locomotives, fed with briquettes, trailed long clouds of smoke. The pitch-black locomotives formed a sharp contrast to the snow-covered land we were crossing and were easy targets for Russian fighter planes. Only the six-foot high slogan "Wheels must roll for victory," which had been painted on the train, blended in with the white all around us. We passed bombed-out houses and farms everywhere. Everything looked like the aftermath of a battle. After the seemingly endless journey, we reached Stettin (today Szczecin), a haven of peace and security, it seemed. Here we were to get to know another aspect of total war. "Air-raid! Air-raid!" Then the night was filled with howling sirens. "Air-raid! Quickly into the air-raid shelters!"

It had become mandatory to go to air raid shelters, as more and more people had ignored this order. Many thought that it was only a matter of time before they were hit anyway. Why try to delay your own death, when it is so difficult to get into an air-raid shelter day or night?

It was Sunday afternoon when I, a stranger in a strange city, had to hurry to safety with a large crowd of people. I was ragged and dirty; then I experienced something totally unbelievable. In one part of the shelter there was a large group of boys and girls who belonged to the Hitler-Youth. They all looked clean and well-groomed—indeed their uniforms were as immaculate as if they were about to undergo a strict inspection. They behaved with exemplary composure. Somehow, I ended up joining them because I felt connected to them, even though I didn't fit in with them due to my neglected appearance. Perhaps it was also the real threat that drew us together. We were confronted by a brutal and insidious enemy who was trying to wipe out the defenseless civilians of the city. While the air-raid shelter shook under the attacks and the sound of the heavy bombs detonating was clearly audible even underground, we began to sing. We sang calmly, beautifully, and harmoniously, convinced that one day we would be rehabilitated and victorious despite the vile attacks of these barbarians. Serious and solemn, our voices drowned out the muffled noise of the bombs impact: "Germany, holy word, thou full of infinity, beyond the ages, be thou blessed.[1] Holy are your lakes, holy your forests, and the garland of your silent heights up to the green sea…" This melody was simply good; it was so solemn and heart-warming. Stettin didn't have anything significant to offer me. The refugee aid was well organized. They tried to help the refugees on their way west without further delay. Although I had no real goal and was a bit lost, I decided to follow their guidance. The train took me to the North Sea port of Hamburg, where I was to get a taste of the destructive actions of the American Air Force. When I left the station in Hamburg, I almost couldn't believe my eyes: As far as you could see—left, right, straight ahead—nothing but rubble. Not even a single chimney had been left standing to remind me of earlier times. Despite this complete

---

1 Gebenedeit—Old word for "blessed."

destruction, the population showed the same stoic attitude that I had already encountered in Stettin: "If this is the price for the final victory, we are prepared to pay it." Life went on as normally as possible—apart from the possibility of an air raid at any time.

You could buy fried flounder in a fish store near the station. Where did they get such a delicacy? The risk of going out to sea was considerable, but the goods were still offered at regular prices.

What impressed me most was the men's restroom at the main station. The white tiles shone immaculately. The windows were also intact, and the water supply had not yet been interrupted. For me, it was a rare sight of order and cleanliness in a collapsing and burning world. I therefore considered it a blessing to visit this place. It reminded me of a past that now seemed far away and unreal. But it was inevitable that one day even this charming picture would be destroyed. I hadn't noticed that a bomb had fallen nearby, but when I went back into the restroom one day, the windows were cracked and scorched. The once shiny tiles were broken and sooty. Water poured from a grotesquely deformed faucet. I had been satisfied with so little, and now even that had been taken away from me! There were new surprises every day.

Since I had met up again with some of the "old boys" from our early days, I no longer felt alone. Among them was a good-natured and daring guy called Weber, who had completed the same training as I. At first, we gave each other a richly exaggerated account of how we had tried to make our way to the West, then we became more serious. None of us felt the urge to return to the Netherlands. We wanted to stay where there was something going on and discussed our options. As we were still not seventeen, we were not eligible for military service. The war was coming to an end, and we had not yet experienced any real war action. There were constant rumors that the secret weapon Hitler had long announced would soon be deployed.

An officer had told me confidentially that he had important insider information: "Soon the world will be surprised." These words sent a tingle down my spine. Victory seemed within reach. Armies and nations that had thwarted our plans for so long would have to kneel before us while our troops marched in long parades. Then the death of the many comrades who had fallen on the Eastern Front finally made sense. But we wouldn't be able to take part in the parade, simply because we had been born a bit too late! That was unacceptable. Our official papers had long since been lost. So, who was going to prove our age? In the confusion of those war days, it was also impossible to check with a registration office. And a little fraud like that, if it benefited our country, couldn't do any harm.

About six of us reported to a Waffen SS recruitment office. Nobody asked us our age when we filled out the required forms and signed up for the entire duration of the war. Without delay, we were assigned to nearby barracks, and we received our uniforms that very afternoon. We had made it! It didn't matter to us that our clothes weren't new. A ten-centimeters-long piece of fabric of a different color had been sewn onto my pants as an extension; there was a patch on one knee. Together with the socks we were also given rags to wrap around our feet. But the most important thing was that my uniform jacket had the SS emblem on it, which I had been chasing after for a long time. It was April 5, 1945. That night there was an air raid, and everyone had to leave the barracks. As I stood outside with my trench coat, with my own helmet and rifle, I felt confident and undaunted. Even the explosive shells whistling past me couldn't change that.

The next morning's training began in earnest. It was short and thorough. Whatever was at hand was thrown into battle to stop the advancing enemy. It seemed only a matter of hours before the Fuehrer would use our secret weapon. A strong premonition of this was already circulating among the young recruits.

After a harsh and rough winter, spring had arrived. With the reawakening of life came new hope. Even among the ruins of the houses, the irresistible forces of nature were breaking through, and it was good to be warmed by the sun's rays, because we had been freezing for months. Almost two years had passed since I had left my home country to build a future in the East. Despite all the setbacks and complications, I never complained. But now came a blow that seemed totally unfair to me. I felt cheated and hit below the belt.

Air raids had their advantages. We lay in a sheltered spot in the sun and calmly watched the silver bodies in the blue sky as the enemy went about their deadly mission. After the "all clear" signal, our strenuous training continued, allowing us to unload our pent-up energy. But after just a few days filled with all kinds of activities, I felt tired and listless. My whole body ached and the prospect of another day at the shooting and training range suddenly held no appeal for me. As I couldn't eat, Weber suggested that I report to the infirmary. The doctor looked me in the eye and didn't need too long to make the diagnosis: Hepatitis. These words made my spirits sink; I was completely desperate. "At least three weeks of complete bed rest," the doctor ordered. Even the prospect of a special diet did not bring me any joy. Within an hour I was in the hospital. I hadn't slept on white sheets for months, but that was of little interest to me. One day, Weber visited me, overjoyed, and told me that our troop had been honored in a special way. The leader of the SS, Heinrich Himmler, had ordered the formation of an elite battalion to fight tanks on the Western Front, and our unit was to take part. This was an opportunity to achieve military honors before the end of the war! But I had to stay in bed during these electrifying and eventful days.

A short time later, our "elite force" set off at night. When I heard about it, I could have cried. Some of them never came back from their first and only mission. They had to learn the hard lesson that enthusiasm alone, no matter how great, is not a sufficient weapon against 52-ton tanks, because the armament had been completely inadequate. When a straggler from another unit later told me about the experience, I was devastated. The hepatitis had probably saved me.

On April 20, all the patients in our ward gathered around a small radio. It was the "Führer's," (Adolf Hitler's) birthday. He had a message for us on this memorable day. I remember this phrase from his speech: "This year, I proclaim to you the final victory of the Greater German Reich." The speech received thunderous applause, followed by resounding marching music. One could almost see the victorious German armies marching in the background. Some older men furtively expressed doubts about the outcome of the war and were therefore sharply rebuked by us. Like many others, I was completely convinced that our victory was imminent, because I wanted and needed to believe it. What would have remained of me if nothing had come of this dream? We stood by the windows of our station and discussed Hitler's words. Canadian and American forces had advanced to within thirty km (eighteen miles) of the military hospital. From our observation post, we tried to find out whether the sounds of war were getting closer or whether the enemy had finally been stopped.

Nobody could believe it at first, but three weeks later it was all over. The incomprehensible had happened. The German army that everybody felt to be invincible had surrendered on all fronts. According to unconfirmed reports, Hitler was dead.

What followed was an overwhelming vacuum. But soon we had to face the reality of life and the fight for survival again. The military doctors tried to keep me in the hospital for as long as possible. When the frequent checks by the Allied Forces in the military hospital made it impossible to stay any longer, I was discharged. Physically weak and mentally depressed, I was sent to a prisoner-of-war camp. Immediately after the news of the capitulation, someone had broken into the barracks, and my few belongings had once again disappeared. I was alone and as poor as a church mouse.

Millions of disarmed men had been rounded up in the northernmost part of Germany. Schleswig-Holstein seemed the most suitable location for a huge prison camp. The Danish border lay to the north. The North Sea in the West and the Balt Baltic Sea in the East formed natural barriers. In the south, the heavily guarded Kaiser Wilhelm Canal made escape attempts seem futile from the outset.

We were welcomed by a delousing committee, where our sleeves, pants and hair were sprayed with DDT.[1] I did not doubt the necessity of this measure, but the pungent smell of this chemical still made me feel sick. Next came a visit to the medical staff, who gave us typhoid vaccinations. Then I was assigned to a hayloft at a nearby farm as a camp, which was already crammed with soldiers lying around in the loose straw and passing the time playing cards.

The food rations were extremely limited. Either there really weren't any

---

1 An insecticide that was banned in Germany in the 1970s.

more rations or the limit was deliberate—I wasn't sure. In any case, hunger remained a constant companion. After the hepatitis, I still felt weak and the daily ration of two slices of bread and a watery cabbage soup was not enough to return my strength. The same was true of my high fever that came after the typhoid injection. Sick and hungry I lay in the straw and gradually began to feel like an animal. When the fever finally subsided, I got up. I found some old, shriveled potatoes by the dung heap behind the barn. I had eaten meals consisting solely of potatoes in the past, but by a stroke of luck I discovered a real bacon rind among the garbage. Young nettles, cooked in an empty tin I had found somewhere, made a wonderful vegetable side dish. I fully enjoyed this hearty, albeit salt-free, meal.

Something inside me resisted captivity, because it was humiliating and dishonorable. When there was still a choice, I often boasted: "I'd rather die than go into captivity." It seemed unfair and humiliating to me to be imprisoned without having had the chance to die.

The timing and nature of our release became the main topic of our conversations. It was clear to me that at least two reasons stood in the way of my early release. Firstly, I was a foreigner who was not expected to be in the camp. Secondly, my voluntary enlistment in the Waffen SS was not exactly a plus. I could understand that the Allies were now trying to take control of all the SS men, because they had proven on many occasions that they were an extremely disciplined and well-trained fighting force. I had always heard rumors about atrocities committed by SS men, but I always rejected them. As far as I had seen, these were much more a reaction to the attacks by the American terrorists.

I was thrilled when the announcement was made that they would soon start breaking up the prison groups. My plan was already set. To ensure that the harvest could be brought in, the farmers were to be released first. I had nothing to lose by trying to play a little game. When the first group of farmers lined up happily and expectantly to be released to go home, I was among them. The inspection was more thorough than I had expected, but I resolved to persevere. Several officers and civilians checked everyone's papers carefully.

Obviously, there were also some foreigners among them.

Now it was my turn. An immaculately manicured hand reached for my (forged) papers.

"Name?"

"Jacques Hubert Teeuwen."

"Place of birth?"

"Haarlem."

"Where is that?"

"In Poland."

"Where do you want to go now?"

I had to give a more detailed answer and now my Dutch accent gave me away. At least that's what I thought. According to military custom, the officer started shouting at me because I spoke such bad German. You wouldn't expect that from a country bumpkin who was born and raised in Poland, he concluded. None of this bothered me. I was happy to put up with all the insults as long as my counterpart continued to believe that Haarlem, the capital of northern Netherlands, was a Polish city. In the meantime, I did my best to look as stupid as possible. The committee had already moved on to the man next to me, which perhaps meant that my case was closed. But I rejoiced too soon. Standing slightly apart from the other questioners, a man in foreign civilian clothes now approached me. He viewed me coldly before looking through the papers that were supposed to be my military ID. "You're a foreigner," he stated, "you're Dutch."

What was left for me to do? Within an hour I found myself back in the hayloft. "But a serious player does not give up after the first try," I told myself. Maybe I'd have better luck next time. A few days later, the next group was called for release. I joined them and hoped fervently that the scary man from last time would not be there. He was, but even when I was waved through, I still felt insecure until the wagon of joking and singing soldiers had left the camp. I was always prepared to be whistled back at the last minute. I helped on a farm for a few weeks. One day, an ambassador from an official organization appeared and told us that all foreigners had to leave as quickly as possible.

Returning to the Netherlands was not as exciting and beautiful as I had imagined. Everyone who came from Germany was viewed with suspicion.

We were questioned by all kinds of committees why we had gone to Germany and what we had done there. I talked openly about my time in Poland, but thought it was better not to mention my involvement in the Waffen SS. The fact that I had gone to Germany as a volunteer did not exactly win me the trust of the authorities, but in the end I was on my way to Haarlem and thought that the interrogations were now over. But lo and behold, another committee met me at the Haarlem station. As it was my hometown, my name was registered. "What are you up to now?" The man looked out from behind his desk but showed no real interest. After moving around the world for so long, this seemed like a rather strange question.

Without hesitation, I answered: "Home, of course!"

Suddenly the man came to life. He looked at me disdainfully. "You no longer have a home. Don't you know that your father is dead?" I didn't know because I hadn't heard anything from home for months. The man grinned, and you could tell he was pleased to break this drastic news to me. He watched me to see my reaction. But if he thought he could have fun with me, he was wrong. After all, I had been trained never to show emotion, because that was considered a sign of weakness.

I just stared back defiantly. "Your mother is a political prisoner," the man added with a sardonic smile. I fervently hoped that my silence wouldn't cause him any satisfaction. I also saw it as a small success that he couldn't find any reason to take me into custody.

It was decided that I should go to relatives. I walked slowly and with dignity through the streets of my hometown. How different the walk of these people was compared to the desolate stride of the refugees! There were flags flying everywhere, but for me personally there was no reason to celebrate. Although I was in the place where I was born, I felt like a stranger. I rang the doorbell in a street I didn't know, but it wasn't answered. Apparently no one was at home, so I went back to the main street and sat down on a low garden border. I rolled myself a fag from cigarette butts I had picked up from the street. When I asked a passer-by for a light, I had suddenly forgotten everything I had learned about hiding emotions. "I've just come home from Germany and found out that my father is dead," came out of me.

"That's really bad," said the man, "I'm really sorry. But I must go now. We have a release party tonight." As the man walked on, I scolded myself for forgetting my lessons so suddenly, and I swore to myself that it wouldn't happen again. Suddenly a wave of desperate loneliness overwhelmed me. There was nothing left to live for, no one and nothing to go to. And I didn't yet realize that this was just the beginning. My sister's friends, who hadn't been home when I first rang the doorbell, took me in for the night. I was now in the house of a widowed woman with her young son and daughter. A few weeks earlier, the woman had lost her husband and a son when they had stepped on a mine while looking for firewood on the beach. So there was grief in this house too, but it was completely different from my own. They didn't complain or moan, but even showed compassion for my situation. They gave me food, clothes, and a bed to sleep in. These people were really the only ones who took an interest in the fact that I had lost my father. When they said: "We know how you feel," I believed them. I knew that they went to church regularly, but I still didn't see any connection between this fact and their behavior towards me.

The unsympathetic man at the station seemed to want to play nasty tricks on me. He had ordered me back there for the next morning, where I had to wait for four or five hours in a crowded office. I was then told to go home and report back the next day. The next day I experienced the same thing again. When I complained, I was given the angry reply: "We've been waiting for you for years. Can't you at least wait a few hours now?"

This way of taking revenge seemed rather childish to me, but I followed the instructions and always came back at the time I was told. I suspected that they were just waiting for me to either not show up or leave before I was allowed to. In that case, they could have easily framed me for trying to escape and locked me up. So I put up with the days of waiting. As they didn't want to release me completely, I was assigned to a home for children up to the age of 12 whose parents were political prisoners. I would have preferred being locked up in jail, but I found the home humiliating. When I arrived at the children's home, I was immediately surrounded by a pack of toddlers with runny noses who stared at me with big questioning eyes: "Daddy? Daddy?"

So after a two-year absence, the seventeen-year-old "Großbauer," assistant to the camp leader and officer candidate, came home and brought all his worldly possessions with him: a rucksack, a sweater, and a pair of socks. That was in July 1945.

On the one hand, the children's home could have been bearable because there was enough to eat, and the caregivers were friendly. For the first time in many months, I experienced something like a routine again. The air raids had stopped.

On the other hand, I was terribly bored. There were no guards or closed gates, yet it was forbidden to leave the premises. I didn't even try, because where was I supposed to go and what was I supposed to do? I tried to make myself useful on the large, neglected estate, which was now full of small children. The extensive, park-like garden needed a lot of attention. Overall, I got along with the caretakers, if they didn't talk about the war or politics.

At that time, "re-education" became an important buzzword. The former Nazis had to be re-educated so that they could be reintegrated into society, and those who were supposed to carry out the re-education were regarded from above as if they were flawless. The whole thing seemed ridiculous and nonsensical. To create the right atmosphere for reeducation, it was necessary for us to show regret about our political affiliation and our participation during the war. This led to totally unproductive and heated debates, because for every argument there was immediately a counterargument.

"How could you cooperate with the Germans, who razed Rotterdam to the ground in one terrible air raid?" we were accused. I could counter that Haarlem had been bombed by the British. I had witnessed it myself, because when I was thirteen, I stood in the burning streets of Haarlem and helped the rescue teams. It was the first time in my life that I saw a dead person. The Germans had destroyed Coventry. But what about Dresden, where in the last days of the war in a single night, around 250,000 civilians were killed? The Germans had many people on their conscience, but the so-called liberators also committed crimes against humanity. My father, for example, although it was known that he had serious heart problems, was forced to walk over to an internment camp after his capture. He collapsed and died. Whether charges and countercharges were always entirely true was not the point. It was simply a matter of working on the opponent until he admitted his guilt. But that was not the right approach, because if there was even a glimmer of insight into one's own guilt, who would have admitted it under such circumstances?

People who had been through the least during the war felt the most compelled to re-educate themselves. But their arguments were too cumbersome for me. I could better understand a communist who admitted to having shot some Germans as a member of an underground organization, because his harshness and cold-blooded hatred were still somehow justifiable. Different laws applied during the war.

I found the church people to be the most boring of all. Nothing upset me more than hypocritical piety. Once, when I was given permission to leave the grounds of the children's home with a supervisor, I met the mother of a former classmate. "So you've come back!" she said without any further introduction. This was followed by several more biting and unfriendly remarks, then she concluded: "And now you'd better come back to church right away, or" she added in an ominous tone, "you'll go to hell like your father." I felt nothing but pity for her.

Another incident was more amusing than hurtful for me. One day there was a commotion in our modest children's home. A religious group had decided to provide the residents of our home with much-needed clothing. A small, select group of privileged children were allowed to take part in the handover. The girls chattered excitedly, and it felt a bit like Christmas. Some children had written down what they needed. Others made guesses about what they would get. When we arrived at the address given, we were ushered into a large, sparsely lit room. In the middle was a box measuring just over a meter long and just as wide. "In the name of Christ our King" was written in bold letters on the page facing us. Several ladies scurried around nervously. Finally, the lid of the box was removed in a solemn manner. Our little gathering fell silent as one of the ladies removed a few items of clothing with great ceremony. It had been made clear to us often enough that we did not deserve the slightest mercy. We only had the kindness of some people to thank for treating us well. Perhaps that was the reason why a gift of clothes that others had thrown away was considered good enough for us. Because everything that the box contained was simply garbage. Actually, I had nothing to complain about. Among the second-hand goods was a new vest. It was easy to imagine how it had ended up here. A well-placed gentleman had bought a three-piece suit and realized after the purchase that he didn't like the vest. Just the thing to pass on in the name of Christ. If I didn't take too deep a breath, it fit like a glove. I also got a woolen scarf, but it was so short that it could hardly be put around my neck and therefore a safety pin was needed to hold the two ends together.

Back at the home, even the twelve-year-olds had to laugh at how "King Christ" had obviously allowed himself a joke with us. A little later, I was to receive further proof of the dishonesty of religious people. The question arose about my future, because I couldn't stay in the children's home forever. Could I continue as a farmer again? The prospects of being able to buy my own farm in the Netherlands were poor and almost hopeless. Besides, I knew now first-hand the hardships of farming life and was no longer sure whether I wanted to pursue this profession for the rest of my life. But with the little formal education I had had, there weren't too many options. What's more, many people didn't want to employ a former Nazi because they weren't sure whether they could trust him.

Because the deputy director of the children's home kindly stood up for me, I got a job in a small local bank. The authorized signatory who hired me was a friendly and helpful man. His philosophy was, "Let's forget the past!" He created opportunities for me to earn extra money, as my regular income had to be handed in at the children's home. I was even allowed to borrow his bike, which was a special privilege because spare parts and tires were hard to come by back then. I was happy about this kindness and was prepared to do my best. I felt safe in our cozy little office. The only snag was that the authorized signatory had hired me without informing the director, who only came in a few times a week. This man had obviously suffered terrible things at the hands of the Germans, so I couldn't blame him for simply not liking me. He never spoke to me beyond what was necessary, but his cold and contemptuous looks said more than many words. A little later, an opportunity to take revenge on me presented itself. An error in the accounts department led to trouble with the head office. Without really knowing what was going on, the director falsely accused me of tampering with the books. He tried to elicit a confession from me. But when that didn't have the desired effect, I was fired.

Losing a job was no longer the end of the world for me. Hadn't my luck run out much earlier? What worried me much more was the fact that the director was known throughout the community as a devout and faithful churchgoer. His hypocrisy confirmed again my conviction that the church people were the least reliable.

I had now lived in the children's home for nine months. The authorities deemed it necessary that I leave the home for my further re-education, and I was sent to a home for young people in their late teens. This home was similar in design to the children's home and could have done with some fresh paint, but the atmosphere there was completely different. I was no longer among children. Most of the young men had been political prisoners or prisoners of war. Others had been badly treated by the Allies, some had been wounded in battle, but all of them had suffered hardships. The caretakers were completely overwhelmed with these young men.

Their priority was to make it clear to us that we were treated much better than we deserved because we were assumed to have been guilty of criminal acts during the war. When unverifiable stories were told about the suffering of unknown people in a faraway land, each of us could come up with personal experiences. Therefore, not much could come out of these discussions except that tempers became heated on both sides.

The second item on the program, for which Mr. and Mrs. X. were constantly present, was to be even more of a flop. The X.s were an unusual couple; they always wore corduroy pants or skirts and checked shirts and blouses. At that time, this was only common for nature lovers, campers, or visitors of youth hostels. Thick, woolen socks and sandals completed her outfit. Mrs. X. also always wore a red ribbon in her tousled hair.

The X.s were peace-loving people, so neither side could count on their support during the war. Re-educating young people in a peaceful and cheerful spirit was something they felt more called to do. They shared their well-intentioned view of life with us: "Forget the past and enjoy the present, because you never know what the future will bring, and you only live once." That was all there was to it. To familiarize us with the practical side of such a noble and carefree way of life, evenings were arranged which we were obliged to attend.

Mrs. X. smiled winningly, while her husband benevolently asked us to let bygones be bygones.

"Come here and form a circle around me!" he exclaimed enthusiastically, but his suggestion was only accepted hesitantly and suspiciously by the self-conscious young men. "What's he up to now?" was written all over everyone's faces. Mr. X. could not be deterred. He smiled contentedly. "I'm going to teach you a new song, an English song. (In fact, Mr. X found that English was a better language for expressing joyful thanks than the German that many of his protégés had spoken for years).

"This nice little song is called 'The Hokey-Pokey'." Mr. X. beamed as if he had just revealed a wonderful secret to us. Someone made a mocking remark, others smiled politely. I made every effort to look as bored as possible. Mr. X. now began to sing:

> "Put your right hand in,
> Take your right hand out.
> Put your right hand in
> And shake it all about
> And dance the hokey pokey
> And turn around
> That's what it's all about."

The second time, Mrs. X. joined in, and finally everyone was invited to sing along, which Mr. X. was delighted with.

"Fantastic! Fantastic!" he shouted in ecstasy. Anyone who thought he was going to call it a day didn't know Mr. X., who had another surprise in store. "We'll sing the whole thing again, but this time we'll move to it," he announced cheerfully.

That was when the circus really began… "Put your right hand in, take your right hand out…"

Mr. X. didn't expect thanks for this beautiful evening. For me, it was a sad reflection when compared to the patriotic songs we had sung with so much conviction. Of course, these songs were now forbidden. Nobody felt like singing anymore.

The best times seemed to be over for good. My home had been confiscated, and my father had been killed. As an additional humiliation, he had simply been wrapped in a sheet (how generous!) and buried in an abandoned, unused corner of the cemetery. Even in death, he was still considered too dangerous to be laid to rest with other people.

My mother was held as a political prisoner for two years. No crime could be proven against her, so at the end of the two years she was sentenced to what she had already served and released. Wasn't this verdict a stroke of genius? It prevented her from claiming compensation. A clever move, there was no denying that, but where was the justice? The very people who behaved in this way pointed their self-righteous fingers accusingly at us "former victims" and accused us of having trampled on the law during the Nazi regime.

Forget the past, enjoy the present? Unfortunately, the people who were assigned to the task of our re-education often had a lifestyle that was repulsive to me.

My bones were still aching from the long time we had to endure the freezing cold on the run from the Russians. My mind was also tired of living. The "Hokey-Pokey" could offer no answers to the ever-growing darkness, loneliness, and despair within me.

It stayed that way for several years, although I must admit that there were opportunities from outside. After about five months in the home for adolescent boys, I was released and from then on lived in a furnished room or with relatives. When my mother was released from prison, I lived with her and two younger brothers in a backstreet in Haarlem.

It was understandable that my mother was inwardly filled with hatred and anger; our home was therefore no longer the same. My own changed condition undoubtedly also played a part.

I found a job in Amsterdam and enjoyed the desk work, but the burning question of whether this was all life had to offer me remained unanswered. Former members of the Hitler Youth met up again, but simply being together without a future perspective was no longer the same. Most, if not all of them, seemed to be better off than me, because they were already building a new future for themselves and encouraged me to do the same.

More as a favor to the others, I started a correspondence course in English, but that only lasted a few months. This was followed by a bookkeeping course, which I also gave up shortly before my final exams. My friends urged me to get more involved in life and find a hobby. To find something to do, I started collecting empty gin bottles, but never got more than half a dozen together, even though I drank so much at times that I lost track of where I was going.

But what good was all that? My bones ached so much that I felt like an old man. The memories of the past weighed on me like a curse, because I simply couldn't forget them. Day and night I was tormented by images of soldiers dying in the snow. I had known many of them personally or secretly admired them.

I couldn't get one picture out of my mind, the first person I had seen dead. It had been a boy, about the same age as me, twelve or thirteen at the time. His head was completely covered in blood. Sand stuck to his hair and, together with the blood, gave him a grotesque appearance. One question settled dull in my brain, "Why? What's the meaning of it all?"

In my despondency, I couldn't find an answer. Even friendships with girls were no solution, although I did plenty of looking around. A former friend from the Nazi era had confided in me: "The only thing that can save us is love with a capital L." I wanted to try, but what could I offer? Since I didn't know what love really was, I couldn't imagine being able to hold my own in this area.

But it couldn't go on like this! For a while I wondered whether I should do what an enemy bullet had failed to do. Like many of my former comrades, I envied those who had died in battle, because at least they no longer had any problems! There was something almost shameful about being a survivor when so many others had lost their lives. "I fell ill at the very moment my battalion left to fight!" Would my peers find that very convincing? Having lived on the brink of death for so long, I no longer feared it. On the other hand, I felt that working out a completely safe plan was just too much effort. The possibility that even a carefully thought-out plan could go wrong was too great. I was aware that in this case everything was much worse than before. You could see examples of this in everyday life.

As a result, my dejection developed deeper and deeper roots until it finally grew into the poisonous fruits of hatred and bitterness. Someone simply had to be the scapegoat I could blame for my misery.

As I tried to find satisfactory answers to the question of the meaning of life, it was quite natural that the question of God also surfaced. No one could accuse me of having given too much thought to a supernatural being in recent years. I didn't like the idea of an all-powerful deity, but I had to grudgingly admit that I often felt as if it was there, whether I cared about it or not. From my childhood, I still carried the image of a grim old man who wanted to spoil my fun. Now this intolerant phantom seemed even more evil. I only had to observe his followers to recognize his ambiguous intentions. They always spoke of love, but they pursued you with hate. "King Christ," charitable donor of new vests and mini scarves, also contributed to this image. Good. Even if I was too powerless to take him on, I wanted at least to take my contempt out on his followers.

FROM THE DEPTH

Jacob could surely not be considered an attractive person. If there had ever been a competition in awkwardness, he could have certainly won. His shock of hair always appeared greasy, his watery blue eyes appeared even bigger through his heavy glasses, and his pale, swollen, and most often poorly shaved face added to his unattractiveness along with his pimples. His lips were too red, and his long fingernails were never clean. His style of clothing did not improve his image. Every day he wore a creased, dark gray-striped and ill-fitting suit. His shirt collar appeared more yellow than white, which led to the assumption that he only owned one shirt. Thick woolen socks showed inside shoes that had never been polished.

Jacob was my younger colleague in the Amsterdam office. We both worked in the accounts department, but Jacob's work was just as messy as his appearance, with all the inevitable consequences. He was simply destined to make mistakes. When he spotted one, he had an irritating habit of letting out a whistle. Sometimes it seemed to me that he would whistle all morning long.

I avoided Jacob as much as possible and even crossed the street when I met him on the way to the office. One reason for this was that he always spoke loudly and unclearly, almost requiring an umbrella for the listener, and he often laughed at his own boring jokes.

Sometimes I reluctantly endured the company of this colleague, because during the lunch break we often played bridge,[1] which required four people that we couldn't always find. So we occasionally resorted to Jacob. In his own way, he was a helpful playing partner, because when the cards were particularly bad, he would whistle to express his disapproval.

One day, we needed Jacob for our game again. The third player also worked in our section but was the exact opposite of Jacob in every respect. He did a good job and always looked immaculately groomed. However, his reports on various drinking bouts were terribly boring. The fourth teammate was Henny, a female secretary who had only been in the office a few weeks. That was all I knew about her, and her looks didn't arouse my interest anyway.

We were in the middle of the game, and I felt a slight excitement because I had a special trump card that day. I don't mean one of the thirteen cards in my hand, but an interesting discovery I had made about Jacob, and it fit my picture perfectly: Jacob was religious. While he sorted his cards unsuspectingly, I made my first move.

"Jacob," I said without any further introduction, "last Saturday I saw you handing out religious literature." Jacob blushed. He looked up, confused and even a little frightened. I smiled condescendingly at him. "Jacob," I said with mock sympathy, "why are you wasting your time with such things? You can't even prove that there is a God."

I played it safe with this argument, because most believers could be silenced with it. Jacob was no different. If his confused stuttering was an answer, no one would be convinced. I had achieved my goal and leaned back with satisfaction to devote myself entirely to the cards in my hand, expecting the game to continue.

But now Henny spoke up. "But I can," she said with a gentle smile. "I can prove that God exists because, after all, Jesus lives in my heart." That was all. Nevertheless, her words hit me like a thunderbolt. Now it was I who was turning red and starting to stutter. Wasn't this ridiculous? I had never heard anyone say a positive word about God before. I had only heard threats of hell, punishment and damnation. But Henny didn't seem as if

---

1 A card game.

she had just said anything sensational, she was just calmly studying the cards in her hand. But I had lost all interest in my favorite game. How could she make such a statement? Religious people are normally loath to talk about their beliefs in public, but Henny was giving information without being asked. I had a strange feeling that this was even worse than an air raid because there was nowhere for me to take cover. I had thought that I had settled all these questions for myself once and for all, and now a girl was saying such stupid things! Where did she get the courage to do that? I felt threatened, although outwardly there was no reason to be. She had only helped Jacob out of a tight spot.

Henny sat there calmly and peacefully while the questions whirled through my head. If Jacob had at least blown his whistle to make it clear that it was a misunderstanding or a joke! I couldn't help it, but I started to take an interest in Henny, even though she wasn't my type. I rather liked feminine, well-groomed and well-dressed women. Although Henny wasn't dressed as horribly as Jacob, of course, she just didn't seem to care what she wore. The natural-colored shoes with the wide straps looked decidedly unflattering. In the office, she wore the usual skirt and blouse combination. For outside, she apparently had nothing but a faded green raincoat with shoulder stripes and a wide belt, in which her petite figure was reminiscent of a very emaciated soldier who had just returned from the battlefield. With a little effort, one could easily imagine that the loose hem of her coat was the result of an encounter with barbed wire.

Nevertheless, there was something about Henny that attracted me. Immediately after that significant game of bridge, I began to show more interest in her. I was pleased to find out that she lived in a suburb of Haarlem, which gave us the opportunity to walk to the train together after work and chat during the three-quarter hour ride home.

In her friendly manner, Henny told me openly about her war experiences. Due to poor health, she had had to abandon her training as a doctor. She originally wanted to follow in the footsteps of her father, who had died in a concentration camp.

The serenity and quiet joy that emanated from Henny impressed me deeply, because I didn't understand her when I thought about everything she had been through. Frankly, I envied her for being able to display her contentment so naturally. I had been taught to hide my feelings, but this wasn't just about hiding them. I wasn't just hiding facts, there was another reality. During a conversation on the way to the train, she suddenly put her hand on my arm and said in a warm voice: "There's always something crying inside you." I was horrified! Had I forgotten my lessons? Nevertheless, I was fascinated that someone could hit the nail on the head with so few words. Perhaps she could also share her secret of joy and happiness with me, because I longed for that very much. But I knew that both were beyond my reach. After all, I was prepared to do anything—let's say almost anything—to get it.

The same thing that attracted me to Henny also alienated me from her. I admired her inner strength and fortitude. She hadn't let the terrible experiences of war get her down. It was admirable how she bore the loss of her father and the resulting poverty without bitterness. But the fact that due to illness she only had a small secretarial job, even though she deserved a higher level, and did not complain, was beyond my comprehension. How did she manage it? What was the key? She obviously had something that I didn't have and that I couldn't get. When the conversation got personal, there was always a dividing line between us. A chasm opened, because whenever we were close to an agreement, Henny would become religious.

"It's Jesus," she said simply, trying to convince me that here was the solution to every problem. I patiently explained to her that I wasn't interested in religion. I rejected God, and to me Jesus was a scary figure with pathetic ideals. I sometimes used his name as a curse, and mocking songs were sung about him in the Hitler Youth. I was only looking for a little happiness in life, not religion. At this point, the otherwise sociable Henny became increasingly stubborn. "It's Jesus," she kept saying, and beyond that there was no discussion for her.

It went on like this for weeks. However, our reactions were different. While I became angry, Henny remained peaceful. The fact that she was so inflexible when it came to religion sometimes bothered me. I wondered if she was trying to pull the wool over my eyes, but her friendly demeanor spoke against it. I therefore concluded that she had not really understood my difficulty and what kind of misery I had witnessed.

One evening, as we were driving home from work, I began to pour my heart out to her. I told her what I had never shared with anyone before; no detail of physical or emotional terror was left out as to how my life had descended into the chaos I was in. It was a long, sad report. When we got to the station where I had to get off, Henny automatically got up and got off with me. We were so caught up in the darkness of my hopeless story that we couldn't go any further. We stood at the station while I recounted my overwhelming sadness. It was the middle of winter; the cold of the snow-covered, frozen ground crept up my legs and made the emotional shock of the past even more vivid. Henny never interrupted me. She just stood there and listened quietly. Eventually I stopped talking. I had confided everything to Henny; I was exhausted and there was nothing more to say.

When I looked at her in the light of the streetlamp, I saw tears running down Henny's cheeks, which didn't happen often. I had only seen her eyes water once before, when she told me how God had shown his love for us by sending his son into the world. This had left me completely untouched. I was even a little impatient because of so much piety. But this was about something else. Suddenly an anxious hope arose in me, and I realized that I had succeeded in penetrating Henny's religious fascination. In the end, she was as vulnerable as other people. I didn't really know how to deal with these mixed feelings and thought that now that I had confided everything to her, perhaps she would also share the secret of her balance and calmness with me. But that turned out to be a very short-lived hope. Henny wiped her tears and said quietly: "I don't know why you had to go through all this." She paused, as if reluctant to share her further thoughts, then continued: "But I know one thing for sure: that Jesus is the answer."

The frozen ground seemed to vibrate under my feet. I suddenly felt numb. All my feelings were blown away and I didn't even feel anger anymore but only total loneliness and emptiness. I had sought understanding and hope and made one last desperate attempt; I had gambled and lost. I knew without a doubt that this would be the last time I shared my innermost experiences and wishes with anyone. Answers were just not possible. Although I was too dazed to feel any emotion, I felt betrayed. For reasons I didn't fully understand myself, I had revealed my innermost feelings to a girl I barely knew, and she had given the superficial and meaningless answer without any empathy, or so it seemed: "I know Jesus is the answer."

Without saying a word, we waited for the next train to take Henny away. When the taillight of the last carriage disappeared into the darkness, my feeling of desolation couldn't have been greater. I walked home through the frosty evening air. Although it was time for dinner, I had no appetite. I retreated to my room where, in utter despair, I first made sure no one was watching me, then knelt and said without much emotion, "Jesus, if you really exist, let me know."

Nothing happened; nothing changed. In fact, I wasn't even waiting for anything to change. I quickly went to bed. At least I had the modest consolation that no one would ever find out how I had let myself go in a moment of great weakness.

The next morning it was still so cold that on the way to the station, the smoke from my cigarette was mingled with my breath. When I entered the carriage compartment, I automatically looked around for Henny, but couldn't see her. The atmosphere was suffocating—the windows were closed, and everyone was smoking. It was like a world that was suffocating itself in smoke and didn't want anyone to escape. How good it felt when we reached Amsterdam, and I could breathe in the fresh morning air again! When I arrived at the office, Henny was already there. I met her on the way to the cloakroom. After we greeted each other, she looked at me penetratingly. Then she said with a questioning look: "You look changed today. Have you been praying?"

Her words did not fail to have an effect. Suddenly it was there again, what I had sworn to myself to forget forever: "Jesus, if you really exist, let me know." I had mumbled that the night before. And really, something had happened. Something had changed. I suddenly realized that I hadn't thought about the war all day. This frightened me at first because, after all, the war was a part of me, something that belonged to me. Now I consciously tried to recall the images that had accompanied me constantly in the seven years since the war ended. But strangely, I suddenly saw everything unfold before me like an outsider. The pain, grief, and horror that I usually felt were no longer there. What I had experienced so vividly in Henny and what I had always longed for had now returned to me: serenity and peace.

Henny was still standing there. "That's what Jesus does," she said. "That's what Jesus can do in you." She beamed.

The day dragged on endlessly. Not even the usual game of bridge held any attraction for me. The whistle that could be heard from behind a certain desk no longer bothered me. In the afternoon, I managed to find an excuse to run an errand. The sun was shining and hesitantly the sparrows joined in a rousing concert. Spring was in the air.

That evening, I went to the station with Henny. I was so changed that for the first time I was able to listen to her without hostility. Not even a quotation from the Bible could upset me. With growing amazement, I realized that Henny was talking about Jesus like a living, dear friend. The tension was broken. It was as if I had escaped a military pincer movement that had almost cost me my life.

When the train reached Haarlem, it was no longer necessary for Henny to get off with me, nor was it necessary to continue the conversation. Even without Henny's presence, I didn't feel alone. Everything was fine—very, very fine. It was February, 1952.

It was not surprising that my knowledge of Christianity was practically nil. What I had previously thought I knew for sure now turned out to be totally wrong. My whole image of God showed my incredible ignorance. Nowhere in the Bible is God portrayed as an ugly, grumpy, and humorless being, as I had heard at school and in the church I had occasionally attended under duress. Rather, the message of the Bible was: "The Lord is merciful and gracious, slow to anger and great in kindness." (Psalm 103:8)

Nevertheless, the negative image of God was so deeply rooted in me that it took weeks before I was ready to face God. It was a wonderful experience when I did it for the first time. Until then, I had been convinced that even if Jesus was good, at least his father had to be evil, because some deity had to be responsible for the evil in the world. Wasn't it an amazing sign of his patience and goodness that he accepted me despite everything? "O depth of the riches, both of the wisdom and knowledge of God! How unsearchable are his judgments and unfathomable his ways!" (Romans 11:33)

Although I had always known that Jesus had been crucified, it never occurred to me that this could have anything to do with me. People simply put on a suitably serious face when it was mentioned. Later, the cross was even mocked in a tasteless way through words and songs. Perhaps someone had once explained the real meaning to me, but I couldn't consciously remember. I learned from Henny that Jesus had personally paid for my sins on the cross and reconciled me with God. Now I could understand why she sometimes shed tears when she talked about these things. But I didn't feel that guilty. There were so many scapegoats who could be responsible for the situation I had been in for so long. I was the only one who could be blamed for the situation I had found myself in.

My knowledge of the Bible was also lacking. I knew that there was an Old and a New Testament. I vaguely remembered the names Peter and Paul, but for a long time I believed that a single man with two names was meant.

During the first few months in which that incomprehensible change had taken place in my life, I was completely convinced that Henny and I were the only people in the world who had such an intimate knowledge of God's love revealed in Jesus Christ. Although in hindsight I don't understand why, Henny seemed to reinforce and support this thinking. I don't remember if the word "evangelization" meant anything to me until then. "Mission" was also a very vague term. Somehow it had to do with the penny we had to take to school every Monday morning "for the heathen nations." A fat preacher had once visited our school and showed us photographs of black-skinned people living somewhere in the tropics. They were "Gentiles," because they didn't know as much about God as we do. Although I still had much to learn, a conviction began to grow in me. My whole way of thinking was transformed: "What God through Jesus Christ has accomplished in your life is so fantastic that you have to go out and tell others about it." It was obvious that those with whom I had experienced so many bad things during the Second World War should be the first people to tell. Henny agreed. Although my plans encompassed the whole world, Eastern Europe and Germany were always my first thoughts. So, we waited for a clue that would show us what to do.

The relationship between Henny and me was no longer limited to the fact that we worked in the same office and shared the same spiritual interests. We had fallen in love and promised to be faithful to each other until death in the service of our Master. It was a happy time we spent together. We were together every day, not only on the train and during office hours, but also in our free time. We read the Bible, prayed and talked with each other. When Easter came, we celebrated in our own little church service. Because, as I said, we believed that there were no other believers like us. For the first time, I understood something about the sacrifice of our suffering Savior and the connection with my own guilt.

The Netherlands is a country with lots of sun and wind, and we enjoyed the wide beaches, the sandy dunes, boat trips on the canals and lakes and cycling tours over fertile, reclaimed land.[1]

In all of this, we did not lose sight of our real goal. We continued to pursue our private studies and our preparations to go out on the mission field. Once, when a crusade was held on the beach, we became aware that there were others who shared our faith after all.

Over time, there was a slight change. I thought a lot about the Second Coming and was convinced that Jesus would return soon—indeed, I was looking forward to it! But could I offer him something if he suddenly came? What was I doing in the office still? It was probably a hidden form of unwillingness that I was still there. Had he already called me, and I had missed his voice? Finally, the desire to share the good news with those people with whom I had experienced the devastation of the war became overwhelming. Some of them still had to live crowded together in refugee camps because it was no longer possible to return to their homeland (the Eastern States, which had now become communist).

So, about a year after I became a Christian, I quit my job rather abruptly. Henny agreed that I would go to Eastern Europe and promised to wait

---

1 Polders—low land reclaimed from the sea and protected by dikes

and see how things would develop. A few days later, she told me goodbye at the train station in Amsterdam.

It was a sobering experience to go out into the world without any visible support. But on the eve of the trip, while leafing through the Bible, I had received a wonderful encouragement from God. "So do not be anxious, saying, 'What shall we eat?' or 'What shall we drink?' or 'What shall we wear?' For after all these things do the nations seek: for your heavenly Father knoweth that you need all this." (Matthew 6:31-32) Strangely enough, these were pretty much the only worries I had. The question of whether I would be spiritually up to my self-imposed task barely crossed my mind.

It came as a shock to me when I returned to the world I had left about eight years ago. The camp I visited was just as overcrowded as the refugee train I had jumped on at the beginning of 1945. The people were just as poor. I watched in dismay as a young girl picked up a red ribbon that was about four inches long and had fallen out of a cardboard box brought by an aid organization. For the girl, the ribbon was as precious as a long-awaited Christmas present. Just like back then, people were eagerly awaiting good news. However, the question was no longer: "When is the train leaving?" but: "When will we finally get out of this camp?" It was understandable that these people also tried to use religion to escape the camp, any religion that seemed to be a possible means of doing so.[1] But after a short time, I realized that no matter how much youthful enthusiasm I had, it was not enough to really help these homeless people. You can know the solution to a problem but to communicate in an understandable way so that the other person can also accept it is another matter, although the refugees were willing to discuss the issues.

Older men with more experience in this ministry kindly pointed out my shortcomings, and I gratefully accepted their advice. I returned to the Netherlands after just a few weeks. But there were two other reasons for this.

Quite unexpectedly, Henny confessed that she had made a mistake with me and dumped me. She never gave a real reason, but I am

---

[1] For example, by accepting God's gift of salvation as a pretense they hoped that the foreign missionary might be able to help them obtain a passport.

convinced that she acted under pressure from outside. It was a devastating blow from which I didn't recover for years. Once again, I had been betrayed by one of His people, but now the circumstances were even more personal. Nevertheless, I did not allow myself to be swayed from my course: Even if everyone should reject me—Jesus never would! Whether I was with someone or alone, I only had the desire to follow Him. As for Henny, I will always be grateful to her for being willing to show me the way to life.

The second reason for my early return was due to a natural disaster that struck the Netherlands. Because of an unusual combination of high tides and extremely strong winds, the water had risen over the dikes and caused flooding in many parts of the country. Dikes had swayed under the violent waves, and thousands of houses had collapsed under the incessant lashing waves, leaving countless people without homes. Around two thousand people were killed.

Help was urgently needed: Accommodation had to be created for the survivors, and food, clothing, and bedding had to be brought to the disaster area to protect people from the extreme cold. Dead people and livestock had to be removed from the water as quickly as possible, the dikes rebuilt, and the salt water pumped out of the flooded reclaimed land—all as quickly as possible. As soon as the water had receded, the plan was to start rebuilding the devastated country.

Aid and rescue teams arrived from countries around the world. It was therefore very clear to me that I should also get involved.

The experiences I had in this context became extremely meaningful for me, because for the first time I realized how immature my own faith still was and how graciously and kindly God nevertheless stood by me and guided me. This became clear to me in various situations that one might have thought were not interesting enough for the Creator of the entire universe.

Due to a lack of money, I was forced to hitchhike back to the Netherlands from Germany. I then spent a few days at home. As I had no money to travel to the disaster area in any other way, I readied my bike for the two-day trip. However, the resulting delay threatened to be my undoing. Whomever I contacted; I got the same answer: "Why didn't you come a few days earlier? We still urgently needed people then! Now we don't need any more." I had been on my bike all day, and everywhere I went I heard the same thing. When it got dark, I asked for accommodation at an undamaged farmhouse. The well-fed, cigar-smoking farmer looked at me suspiciously, but eventually allowed me to spend the night in the hay.

The next day was cloudy and foggy. I tried to give a testimony to my hosts, but their two school-aged children mocked me, which their parents found funny.

As I moved on, I felt uncomfortable, hungry and cold. When I went to the office, I was once again rebuffed: "Why didn't you come a few days earlier when we urgently needed people? We don't need anyone now!" I cycled away along the dike. An abandoned house stared out through its crooked shutters at the water lapping at its feet. Why wasn't anyone renovating the house? Suddenly I felt angry at all these well-fed, cigar-smoking, giggling people sitting in well-heated offices who wouldn't let anyone help. There wasn't a soul around, so I had to take out my anger on God. After all, wasn't He responsible for this misery? I was still pious enough to close my eyes, but not enough to get off my bike, so I prayed while cycling with my eyes closed.

"Lord, if you want me to be here, how come I can't find any work?" I pressed him. Another short scolding followed. But fortunately, my prayer was cut short. When I opened my eyes, I was on the wrong side of the road and heading straight for the cold water at the foot of the dike. I quickly corrected my course. A motorcycle appeared in the distance. As it got closer, it slowed down, and I wondered if it was a policeman who was going to stop me for drinking and driving. The motorcycle stopped. "Call number nine in Tholen, there's work for you there!" the driver shouted to me over the noise of the engine—and then drove off again.

I quickly went to the nearest telephone and dialed nine. When someone answered on the other end, I made my request. I couldn't believe my ears! "Why didn't you come a few days earlier when we urgently needed people? Now we have nothing free," a male voice replied. I could almost smell the cigar smoke through the line and imagined my counterpart sitting comfortably in a warm room. But the voice gave me another address where I could make an inquiry. So, the next morning I was sitting in a well-heated office calculating wages for the dike workers. I was provided with food and accommodation. When someone offered me a cigar, however, I declined.

My contribution to the reconstruction of our destroyed country was hardly worth mentioning. However, I had had another important and sometimes shameful prayer experience, and I hope I learned something from it.

THE OCCUPATION

About six months later, my work in the office came to an end as most of the repair work on the dikes was finished and the number of people calculating wages for the dike workers was reduced accordingly. I returned to Haarlem and tried to enroll in a Bible school program over the summer, but without success. So, I took the advice of some experienced Christians and looked for a job. A short time later, I was taken on as a "jack of all trades" by a company that made machines for peeling potatoes and cutting vegetables. Although I was now back in a secular job, my desire to serve the Lord was still there.

Until then, I had been a bit of a loner when it came to Christian fellowship. I occasionally took part in conferences that were held at irregular intervals. I rarely went to church, simply because I didn't know of any community where I could feel at home. One day I was leafing through the newspaper when my eyes fell on the name of an evangelist who had led a beach outreach a few years earlier. It was said that Mr. Pasman would be speaking at the *Zuiderkapel* in Haarlem. I had never heard of this place before, but since Mr. Pasman had made a good impression on me at the time, I thought that I might meet like-minded people in *Zuiderkapel* Street.

The next Sunday I attended the service there and was not disappointed. I found a warm community of believers singing joyfully about their "Jezus alleen" (Jesus alone). These words were also written on the front wall of the somewhat dilapidated building. It was formerly a movie theater, to which a sign in front still gave witness.

I was warmly welcomed and soon felt at home among these enthusiastic Christians. Mr. Pasman was one of the regular guest preachers, and one day I plucked up the courage to come to him with some of the many questions that were bothering me. He proved to be a patient listener and wise counselor. In the end, he promised me that he would help me get a place at the German Bible school, where he himself had been, if I took part in the activities of the *Zuiderkapel* for a year and proved myself. I was thrilled, because a German education would be a great preparation for my ministry among the refugees.

I wholeheartedly took part in the church's program and, without knowing it, embarked on a greater commitment in my life. Despite all my immaturity and lack of knowledge, I could seriously say that I loved Jesus. He was with me in everything I did, and I talked to Him like a friend. Reading His Word wasn't an obligation to me, because everything was so new and experiencing His love was so invigorating. How had I been able to live without Him for so long? When I studied the Bible, I could not deny that, apart from what he had done for me, there was also a very clear and undeniable question. Jesus Christ had given everything for me—how much was I willing to do for him?

I had already been confronted with this in the first few months after becoming a Christian. I had said rather superficially and thoughtlessly: "Everything that is mine is mine, and everything that is mine is His." But apparently the Lord had taken me at my word. I kept thinking about a certain amount of money that I had put aside to buy a new coat. I couldn't get the thought out of my mind that Christ wanted this money. If it was mine, it was also His. The thought made me uncomfortable. Even if I was prepared to give the Lord the twenty-five guilders, I still didn't know a concrete way to do it. I had been amused by the talk of a man who jokingly said: "Every month I take my salary and throw it into the air. What stays up belongs to God, and what falls I keep." I just didn't know where to put my offering. In the end, I decided to put the money in the

Salvation Army box that was set up on the street for the annual collection. After I had done this, my peace of mind returned. I didn't speak to anyone about this incident, but three days later a friend confided in me that he had won the lottery and gave me seventy-five guilders. That was more than enough to buy the coat I needed. This was not to be the last time that God provided for me in an unusual way.

But apparently there was more at stake here. Jesus Christ didn't just want my money or my time—He wanted me. When I realized this, it wasn't difficult for me to agree. After all, what was I without Him? He had given me new life, new hope, and a new purpose in life. Not long after my conversion, He had also freed me from my agonizing bone pain.

One day I was sitting all alone and had the Bible open in front of me when I prayed sincerely and joyfully: *"Lord Jesus, I belong to you. I am ready to do all You want. I am ready to go anywhere you want me to go. If you want me to write, I will write whatever you want me to write."* Here I stopped and thought that a small caveat would be reasonable: *"Anything, except to become a preacher. I don't think I could stand up front and have hundreds of eyes staring at me."*

The youth group of the *Zuiderkapel* consisted of active young people who, out of a strong and enthusiastic first love, gave witness to their faith wherever possible. Their zeal was so infectious that people were happy to join them. If the whole world was to know, why not start in Haarlem? Every week small groups of young people swarmed out, going from door to door and handing out small tracts with Bible verses. After each outreach, the respective streets were marked on a street map to ensure that none were overlooked. We also noted which houses had reacted positively to our visit. One group had planned to visit the bars on Saturday evenings to talk to visitors about questions of faith. Our dedication was great—but whether we had the right approach remained to be seen.

During the summer months, we held our meetings outdoors. "De Dreef" was the name of a beautiful and lively walkway not far from the city center. It was run by a Mr. Sussenbach, who came from Surinam, was short in stature, and very dark. He was a factory worker, but everyone admired him for his knowledge of the Bible and his thoughtful yet direct way of addressing those who stopped to listen. He also had a fine way of dealing with Christian workers—both adults and young people. At the meetings, songs were sung first, then Mr. Sussenbach gave a short message. This was followed by another song, after which he stepped down from the park bench from which he had been speaking. One could imagine him praying as he paced within our group and then approached one or two who were to speak next to the expectant crowd. It was unrealistic to expect that it would never be my turn. And one day Mr. Sussenbach came up to me. He just said my name and put a question mark after it: "Jacques?"

There was no escape. His friendly dark eyes showed me that he would not accept "no" for an answer. And then, what would the other young people think if I refused? Although I knew that was not a valid excuse. So, I nodded in agreement with Mr. Sussenbach, but when I stepped out of the group and stood on the park bench, I was at a loss for words. Dozens of eyes were fixed expectantly on me. The singing behind me came to an end. I felt dazed and confused; then the title of the last song I had sung took shape inside me. It became the first sentence of my first speech: "I know that my Savior lives," I shouted as loud as I could across the walkway. That was all I could think of. But it also became a key, because suddenly my mind was working again. The spell was broken, and I told in simple words what Jesus had done for me. That was the first time I had stood in a "pulpit," and it was not to be the last. That park bench became a place where I regularly shared the Word of God.

I began to enjoy speaking in public. To this day, I consider this gift to be a miracle of God's grace. The fact that I have now preached the Word of God in five languages and, with the help of many translators, on all continents, does not change my attitude of grateful dependence.

The young people of the *Zuiderkapel* asked me to regularly attend their Sunday evening meetings. I believe that I learned at least as much from these evenings as the young people did. So, a whole year flew by.

But there was something else I had to learn during my time as an apprentice in Haarlem. What Jesus had accomplished as the firstborn from the dead with His resurrection was incomprehensible to me in human terms. I only really understood part of it through the gripping story of a preacher whose name and appearance I had forgotten long ago. He compared the human situation to an air-raid shelter which, because of a direct hit, was buried by fallen debris. The people in the air-raid shelter were all alive, but there was no way of escaping this terrible prison. They were trapped and isolated from the outside world. Every attempt to dig an escape route failed. Everyone was lost because no one could reach the air-raid shelter from outside. It was unimaginably dark down there, and the mood was even darker. Suddenly, sounds from the unreachable world outside penetrated, and a new, still vague hope began to stir. Suddenly a bright ray of sunlight broke through the darkness. Where death had reigned seconds before, confidence now arose. Minutes later, hope became certainty and a triumphant voice called out: "Someone is already out!" And if one could escape, the others would too.

Since I had experienced both—the horror of the air raids as well as the fact of the resurrection—this metaphor left a deep impression on me. When I realized how God in Jesus Christ had opened the gates of death to set me free, all my hatred and bitterness was gone, and I no longer had any difficulties with those who had treated me so incredibly unjustly under the cloak of justice. I could forgive the man whose insensitivity had caused my father's death. Material goods that had been stolen or lost had been replaced; besides, these things were only temporary, and I wasn't that interested in worldly possessions.

But there was one thing that still gnawed on me and poisoned my inner self. I lived in peace with all people—with one exception. I looked back on the war years calmly and told myself: "War is war. If they hadn't caught you, it would have been the other way around." That seemed fair to me, whoever the others were. But this theory failed when it came to the American air force pilots, against whom I harbored deep and passionate hatred. To me, they embodied the vilest cowardice imaginable. I felt abysmal contempt for them.

The last weeks of the war—how could I ever forget them? US bombers flew over us day and night. That wasn't the main problem. Although we were often afraid, we were only defiant when we were shot at by low-flying planes. Their nastiness was that most of them flew above the range of the

FLAK (Flieger-Abwehr-Kanonen or German anti-aircraft artillery guns) and the few remaining German fighter planes. Often you could neither see nor hear them, but from time-to-time white contrails told us of their presence. Or you could see the white lines of falling bombs. Hitting a specific target this way was not possible and probably not intended. The intention was simply to create fear and terror, but in this respect the attacks did not have the desired effect. The only result was even greater hatred on the part of the affected population, and I shared these feelings.

Months after the end of the war, when I encountered American Air Force men for the first time, I had a strong urge to physically attack them. After I became a Christian, these feelings remained in the background, but had not completely disappeared.

A crisis arose when an event was announced in the *Zuiderkapel*. Some Americans had come to the Netherlands to evangelize. This idea seemed a little strange to us, because after all, we were a Christian nation. But it was something special to have foreigners among us, so it was not surprising that our hall was filled that afternoon. Despite the foreign language and their American style of dress, we soon realized that our visitors were happy children of God. What could not be conveyed by words was made up for by songs and warmth. It really amazed me that people could be so relaxed and at ease when several of the group gave testimony. They all had at least one thing in common: the Lord Jesus Christ had made them new people and given them a purpose in life.

Now a young, impressive couple came forward. The girl was pretty, blonde and well-groomed, but her husband, who towered a good deal over her, attracted even more attention. This tall, handsome man with a high forehead, bright blue eyes, and blond hair was beaming with joy. "Hi," he said, flashing a row of white teeth. I hadn't thought that a word consisting of just two letters could express so much. My command of English didn't extend much beyond that word at the time, so I was relieved when the translator began his introduction. "Our guests today are Gordon and Muriel Blythe."

The young man simply stood at the front and smiled as if a wonderful secret had just been revealed. "Gordon was a member of the American

Air Force," the translator continued, "he flew forty-four missions against Germany during the Second World War."

I was shocked. How could such a fascinating man have been a pilot in the hated war machine? And he even had the nerve to smile while this statement was made! Why was he grinning like that? I thought to myself that he couldn't be a real Christian, because my friend Jesus would probably not accept such a man. I was totally baffled. How had this man managed to win me over? I stood up with a jerk, left the room and stormed outside. I can't remember how many times I circled the block before I could begin to think normally again.

First, I argued with God about the choice of his followers. How could he choose a man with such a history? But of course, it was just his background; maybe the man had changed. Slowly that dawned on me. I had perhaps less reason to be proud of myself, but God had accepted me anyway. Although the word didn't sit well with me, I had to admit that I was a sinner—perhaps even a worse one than this Gordon—and yet the holy God had forgiven me. Shouldn't I, a pardoned sinner, also forgive a fellow human being? Great peace came over me when I decided to forgive and accept him.

I went back into the church. Although it wasn't part of the program, I stood up in the middle of the service, stepped out of my row and walked straight up to Gordon. "Brother," I said in Dutch, "I love you in the Lord!" Gordon smiled but didn't understand because he didn't understand Dutch. A translator stepped forward, and I described what I had experienced that afternoon. As Gordon listened to the story, his serious blue eyes filled with tears. Then he said the wonderful words, "Jacques, I too love you in Jesus Christ." I had no doubt about the sincerity of his words. We embraced in front of the whole congregation.

A few weeks later I was a guest of Gordon and Muriel. We didn't talk much about the war, but more about our Lord Jesus Christ. Nevertheless, we found out that Gordon had flown his bomber over Stettin and Hamburg at the same time I had been in those cities. However, this information was no longer a problem for me, but contributed to the fact that we both could not marvel enough at our great and wonderful God.

When the time finally came for me to say goodbye to the *Zuiderkapel* to go to Bible school in Germany, an older couple from the congregation refused to attend the farewell ceremony. "We are not in favor of our church sending out a Nazi," they argued.

Fortunately, God's ways are not the ways of men. It often takes us a long time to realize that He doesn't favor any one person. In any case, I was regularly chosen by my church to teach personal lessons on repentance. However, these exhortations brought no significant success because they came "from above." What people had failed to do, the Word of God finally accomplished, but not overnight.

I had been a Christian for about seven years and had already finished Bible school when I attended a small Brethren meeting in London. The speaker was expounding on the second chapter of Romans; my thoughts were not there, but were drawn to a passage he had read earlier: "Or do you despise the riches of his kindness and patience and longsuffering, not knowing that the kindness of God leads you to repentance?" (Romans 2:4)

I had probably read these words before, but it was only at that moment that they became vivid and meaningful to me. The great gulf that stood between God's goodness and my failure shocked me to the core. Suddenly, I was free from human pressure. The church members wanted to force repentance on me, so to speak. But now I didn't want to continue to resist. I realized that I had unconsciously resisted not only people, but God as well.

Although I had sometimes told the Lord that I was sorry, I had not really repented. Now I could see what God had done for me in His goodness. Jesus was hanging on the cross for me, and not just as a historical figure who had a specific task to fulfill there. Never before had this fact affected me so personally, and this touched me deeply. It taught me that every single person was an object of God's goodness and love. This insight shattered racial and political barriers. God was not simply against the Nazis and for the Allies. Now I struggled, knowing that I had even voluntarily wanted to take part in this absurd destruction of people. I was ashamed of it, and this feeling of unworthiness in comparison to God's goodness has become even stronger over the years, especially when I realize the horror, humiliation, separation, pain, hunger, and fear of death that millions of

God's creatures have experienced. I shudder when I think of what people can do to each other. Everyone was guilty, everyone was lost, and I along with them. God's goodness alone shows us a way out. "Father, forgive me," is not a thoughtless prayer or an easy way out once you understand some of what it has cost God. How can we ever thank God enough for His goodness?

The small village of Wiedenest is located around sixty kilometers (about thirty-seven miles) east of Cologne and is surrounded by pine forests. This hilly area is known as the Oberbergisches Land. In those days, the small wagons pulled by a smoking, huffing and puffing locomotive took quite a long time to cover this distance. But what does time mean? At every stop, the good-natured engineer has acquaintances and takes the opportunity to exchange greetings and news. The shrill whistle of the locomotive, the ringing of the bell and the sudden jolt that hits all the carriages like a wave indicate that the journey continues. There is still enough time for passengers who want to stretch their legs in the fresh country air to get back on board before the carriages groan and start moving again. After many stops, the train finally comes to a halt with a squeak.

"Wiedenest! Wiedenest!" shouts the train driver loudly and emphatically. Wiedenest! I leave the train and enter a world I know from hearsay and picture postcards. A white-painted church dating back to the ninth century on the banks of a shallow but fast-flowing river indicates the place where Wiedenest began. Nearby is a spring, from which an abundance of ice-cold, clear, and tasty water bubbled, attracting weary hikers with its incessant splashing from the rocks below. Legend has it that anyone who has ever drunk from this refreshing water will always return to Wiedenest—wherever they are in the world.

The Bible school is located just a few hundred yards from that source. The whitewashed main buildings and stables once served as a place where travelers could quench their thirst with something stronger than spring water. Hearty meals were also offered. In 1919, the building complex was purchased and rededicated as a Bible school with the aim of educating people, especially from Eastern European countries. While the village of Wiedenest was rural and quiet, the Bible school was more like a beehive in the middle of summer: it was always full of activity. Although the school was not large, it was known far and wide. Seminars and conferences were held outside of school hours, attended by visitors from all over the world.

When I joined the school in 1955, Erich Sauer was the principal: a stocky man in his mid-fifties who was a role model for everyone who met him. He wore very thick glasses and was almost blind; nevertheless, he was always in an excellent mood. During my three years in Wiedenest, I never saw him get angry or lose his temper. We affectionately called him "Uncle Erich", and we were not a little proud of the fact that he was also a world-renowned scholar. His books "The Dawn of World Redemption," "The Triumph of the Crucified," and "From Eternity to Eternity," to name but a few, have been translated into many languages.

From the very beginning, it was clear to me that Wiedenest had more to offer than just clear, sparkling spring water. What flowed even more abundantly was the water of life. The "solid food" of the Word of God, which was offered in generous portions, far surpassed anything that the owner of the "Gaststätte an der Olper Straße" (restaurant in the Olper street) could ever serve his most demanding customers.

I spent three unforgettable years in Wiedenest. Erich Sauer's bubbly personality and excellent lectures alone would have been worth it, but there was more. I had never lived in a Christian community before, and now I experienced the very clear difference from life in the barracks. Every day, we soaked in the Word of God taught by qualified teachers. And sometimes it was also necessary to unlearn things. As we lived quite closely together with other Christians, there were often points of friction, which helped us to hone our character and correct our own behavior. Friction also has the effect of polishing. By applying the lessons of the school to daily life, unexpected strengths of character sometimes came to light.

Most of the students were active Christians. After their time in Wiedenest, many of them followed through on the promise: "To do everything and go wherever the Lord wants to use us." This mission concept was completely new to me. I can't explain why I hadn't heard about it before.

False notions of rotund old men in tropical helmets being chased by lions probably stopped me in my tracks. But here were dedicated young men and women who were determined to take the testimony of Jesus Christ into all the world. Although I was no longer one of the youngest, nor one of the best educated, my enthusiasm made up for what I lacked. Whenever a missionary visited the school and introduced us to a mission field, I went to my room and prayed: *"Lord, I am prepared to go wherever you want me to go."*

You could call this attitude naive; in any case, it caused quite a bit of confusion in my mind. Nevertheless, I still believe today that availability and openness are indispensable prerequisites for experiencing divine guidance. God knows what is in our hearts and can make something out of the chaos, which is very good. For me, this whole process of selection was part of his guidance. The *Zuiderkapel* in Haarlem was used by God to send out a whole host of missionaries to the harvest fields. One of the first to be sent out was Elze Stringer, who was working in "Irian Jaya." I didn't know Elze personally, but her parents and several of her brothers and sisters regularly attended the services in the "Zuiderkapel."

It was perhaps because of this connection that I was sent the "Pioneer," a magazine published by the Christian missionary association that had sent Elze. One issue reported that a CAMA (Christian and Missionary Alliance) pilot named Al Lewis had crashed and died in the interior mountains of New Guinea. I was very impressed by this man's willingness to lay down his life. Almost instantly I prayed the following: *"Lord, there is a gap because of this accident. I am not a pilot, but if I am to fill this gap, I am ready to go."* The death of Al Lewis helped to awaken my interest in New Guinea.

Several former students from Wiedenest had been sent to Pakistan, where the Bible school took on the function of a mission center. With growing certainty some classmates also felt called to Pakistan. I felt a gentle pressure to join them, which was both flattering and reassuring for me. It would certainly be more pleasant to be able to work with classmates in the future than to be completely on my own. It therefore didn't take much persuasion for me to join the prayer group with Asia as its destination. After all, New Guinea was also in Asia. What was a little harder to explain was the fact that I was in a photo showing future candidates for Pakistan, because I had never really confirmed that this was the place God wanted me to be. Something decisive still had to happen for me to be sure which of these two countries I should go to. Or maybe there was another possibility that I had not paid enough attention to? But these questions did not yet cause me sleepless nights, because I was only in my first year of study and was convinced that God's guidance would be revealed by the time I graduated in 1958. To my own astonishment, however, God decided to reveal his plans to me when I had only been studying in Wiedenest for six months.

On the 8th of April, 1956, students who saw their special mission in Africa organized a missionary evening. Many preparations and prayers preceded this meeting. Stage fright and a burning heart for a continent in such need worked together, and they took their responsibility seriously. In addition, all the teachers as well as guests from the local area took part. The fact that the entire student body was present, most of whom were not reserved in their criticism, was another reason to do their best. As the evening approached, the students did very well. We followed the presentation in good spirits and with casual interest. "Let them sweat a little," was intended to illustrate our detached attitude, "after all, everyone gets a turn." That evening, it became clearer to me that the whole world should be our field of work.

At thirty-three, Friedhelm Nusch was the oldest male student at the school. He had given up a thriving printing business to become a missionary. He was in the "world" and yet was prepared to accept the uncertainties and hardships of a life on the mission field instead of material security. Many secretly admired him for this, but for two other reasons he was the envy of others. For one thing, Friedhelm was married, and for another, he already knew where God had called him. On that mission evening, Friedhelm gave a testimony and told in his engaging and casual way how God had shown him that he should go to Africa. He cited gratitude for what God had done for him as his main motivation for wanting to become a missionary. With an inexplicable love and care for a people he had never seen before, he felt called to Tanzania. His devotion to Christ urged him to win these people for Jesus.

Suddenly it flashed through my mind: what he said about Tanzania I could say about New Guinea. The next thought ran through me like a bolt of lightning: *"Then it is New Guinea!"* It came to me so clearly that there was no doubt. I almost couldn't sit still. I felt the urge to rush forward and shout to the congregation with overflowing joy and certainty: *"The Lord has just called me to New Guinea!"* But such things were simply not done in Wiedenest, so I remained seated and tried to look at the matter rationally.

"Don't fool yourself," I said to myself. *"Why should God call you to Asia when he has just called somebody to Africa?"* That was logical. *"Besides, you are just a beginner. And do you know anybody who was called in his first year?"* I couldn't think of any. *"You've already made mistakes,"* the argument continued. *"Do you want to make yourself look stupid before all these people?"*

I therefore decided to stay in my seat and first make sure that God had really spoken. What else was said that evening and what was done passed me by. I eagerly awaited the final prayer, because immediately afterwards I would be able to ask God in silence what it all meant.

When the last churchgoers had left, I pulled an armchair from the auditorium and sat down in the small entrance hall. No one would disturb me there. I intended to stay there until I realized whether God had really spoken. I knelt in front of the armchair and bowed my head. But what was it? Before I could ask a question, words of praise and gratitude came spontaneously and bubbling over my lips—straight from my heart. There was nothing to ask; I could only thank God for the certainty He had given me. He had spoken. He wanted me to go to New Guinea. My joy was complete!

The following night, I woke up at an unusual hour, full of fear. I had probably been dreaming. I saw a vivid and clear image before me: tribesmen from New Guinea, naked and dirty. They were primitive murderers who did not shy away from attacking and killing missionaries. I felt a shudder as the clear and unmistakable thoughts came back into my head: *"You are a hypocrite. You have always maintained that you would go anywhere. And now God has really spoken, and you want to pull out."* Fear mixed with unwillingness. *"Lord Jesus,"* I prayed, *"you are right. I am afraid and already want to give up. But if you want me to, I will go."*

Faster than a lamp lights up when you flip the switch, joy returned to me. Since that night, I have never once doubted that God had called me to New Guinea. This rock-solid certainty was good for me, because it was another five and a half years before I could leave for New Guinea. In fact, dozens of doors slammed shut that could have given me access to New Guinea. The very next morning, I got a taste of what was to come. We were sitting in the classroom waiting for the first lesson. When I heard the teacher coming, I went to meet him outside the classroom to intercept him. "Last night the Lord called me to New Guinea," I blurted out. But there was neither a smile, nor a question, nor a word of encouragement. "We'll see," was all he said, and with that he walked to his desk.

One rule at the Bible school: no friendships between girls and boys during the school year. Preparation for the mission field was considered a priority. Those who were too busy finding a partner would perhaps neglect studying the Bible and lose sight of the essentials. Of course, there was a lot of discussion about this rule, but it was nevertheless accepted by most. The students liked to remind each other of this. No sooner had you had a discussion with a member of the opposite sex and a fellow classmate whispered jokingly, "No flirting, please."

As it turned out, I was one of the few who would make an exception here. After completing the second year of my studies, I was sent to England for the summer months to learn the language. Through the Bible school, I was sent to the Bailey family farm in Wimborne, Dorset. Their daughter, Daphne, and her husband, Rudi, also lived in the old, spacious farmhouse. It was a wonderful, unforgettable summer. In the mornings I devoted myself to my studies, and in the afternoons, it wasn't difficult for me to lend a hand on the farm. Mr. and Mrs. Bailey were in their mid-fifties and a lovely couple: hospitable, warm, and cheerful Christians. Time passed far too quickly, and only a few weeks remained before I returned to Wiedenest to complete my final year of school. It had been such a carefree summer that even "dating" had not been a temptation. I hadn't even thought about it, for one very simple reason: I could only imagine marrying a Dutch or German girl. Somehow, however, an English girl didn't seem to be an option for me. That changed very quickly when Ruth appeared on the stage.

One day, she simply turned up at Honeybrook Farm. She accompanied Rosemary, the Baileys' eldest daughter. Ruth was an attractive person with a gentle character. Her background was also interesting. As the daughter of a state tax inspector, she was born in Haifa, Israel, where she had lived until the age of fourteen. More specifically, her ancestry was not English but Scottish, although she had never lived north of the border. She came to England with her parents at the end of the Second World War, finished school and went on to study theology at St. Michael's College, Oxford.

However, in deference to her father's traditional views, she dropped out of theology studies a year before graduation and began teaching. I thought about it: she was pretty, intelligent, and well-mannered . . . and therefore probably not for me. So, I didn't have high hopes. But why couldn't I stop thinking about her?

When Ruth showed interest in me, too, I initially thought she was trying to make fun of me. Nevertheless, we got on well. When the conversation got too complicated, I switched to German, which she understood well but didn't speak. By using two languages, we were able to converse effortlessly. And then we both realized that we had fallen in love.

A few days before I was due to leave England again, I asked Ruth if she wanted to marry me. When she said "yes," I couldn't believe it at first, as my proposal had included a condition. I had told Ruth about my past and my intention to go to New Guinea. I also had to tell her that God and my calling would always have priority in my life. Ruth would never be able to claim more than second place.

At that time, we had known each other for less than a month, and Ruth could only visit Wimborne on weekends. Today, almost forty years have passed, and she still takes place "number two," something she has never complained about. That's the kind of woman my Ruth is!

Once that had been clarified, I could leave England with peace of mind. But how should I face the director of the Bible school in Germany? Back in Wiedenest, I realized that it wasn't right to circumvent the school's guidelines. I told Ruth about my decision, so we didn't write to each other for four weeks.

Encouraged by a letter from Daphne Bailey in England, I approached the deputy principal. As casually as possible, I tried to explain to him that I had fallen in love, with the emphasis on the fact that it was something that had not been planned.

I found far more understanding than I had expected and was overjoyed to be allowed to write to Ruth. Immediately after this conversation—after a long interruption—I wrote to Ruth. I still consider it a gift from God that I was always able to find a stamp for my daily letters despite my difficult financial situation.

During Christmas vacation in 1957, I spent a week with Ruth in England. At the time of Easter in 1958, she came to Holland for a few days, and on April 6th we bought engagement rings. That was exactly two years to the day after God had called me to New Guinea. We were then able to spend another three weeks together.

A month later, I graduated from the Bible School in Wiedenest and returned to England to attend a course at the Summer School of Linguistics. The course ended on September 19th. On September 23rd, Ruth and I got married in the beautiful little town of Wimborne Minster. After a short honeymoon, we traveled to London and began medical training at a missionary school on October 2nd. The medical terms seemed like a foreign language to me at first. After nine months of hard work, we both passed our exams and won prizes. One of the nicest compliments I ever received was from one of the teachers there: "A year ago he hardly knew any English, and now he's even won a prize."

We had now completed our training and were ready to leave for New Guinea any time.

DEPARTURE FOR IRIAN JAYA

However, this moment was to drag on. Five long years of waiting and testing lay ahead, and time and again our plans were thwarted—not least by rigid missionary authorities.

I held a letter in my hand that had just landed in our postbox and was at a loss as to what to do next. "Listen," I said to Ruth as I read it to her:

>Dear Mr. Teeuwen!
>
>Thank you for your letter, which was forwarded to me by the General Secretary. I am supposed to forward to you the decision made by our counsel. We cannot issue an approval for work in New Guinea. You will easily recognize why we can't encourage you in this.
>
>First, your age speaks against pioneer work in missions. We work generally with missionaries who are considerably younger. Second, we are under the impression that your wife does not have the benefit of Bible school training. Third, because of the huge distance, the travel expenditures between England and New Guinea, not only because of your getting there, but also because of home visits, are exceedingly expensive. Fourth, before our counsel sends somebody to the mission field, we

desire to be well acquainted with them, which is not the case with you.

We are confident that you can accept this decision as from the Lord and are sure that He will reveal to you the desire He has for your life, if you ask Him for that.

Thank you for your interest.

With kind Christian greetings,
    Sincerely,
        The Secretary for Application.

Ruth always tried to see the positive side of things. "At least they answered," she said calmly. How right she was. We had written countless letters to various missionary societies, but many didn't even bother to reply. One missionary society kept us in suspense for two years. Then the decision was made, but when the reply arrived shortly after my thirtieth birthday, we felt like we were being taken for a ride: "Our age limit for candidates is thirty," they wrote to us, "and as you are already over thirty, we cannot accept you." I wrote back that I had not even been twenty-eight when I first applied and therefore could not accept this reason for rejection. We were then told that we had been accepted by the Dutch branch of the missionary society, but that the American committee had yet to approve our application.

While we were in England for a few studies, we were informed that the American personnel manager would be visiting Holland and that we would have the opportunity to meet him. We therefore skipped a few lessons and booked a cheap overnight flight to Holland. When we arrived at the mission office, we had to wait for several hours while other candidates were interviewed. It was already late when our meeting time arrived. "The personnel manager wants to communicate to you that there is no point in talking to you. Because of your age, you don't meet our requirements," the Dutch secretary told us stiffly. And that was all—as far as we were concerned. A little later, we received another letter from the same missionary organization offering us a job in Africa. However, we no longer wanted to work with this group. We politely declined without explaining how illogical this offer really was.

At least the letter I now held in my hand was a clear answer this time. But could my age really be an obstacle when God had spoken? Also, why did they assume that Ruth didn't have a biblically sound education? She had a better one than me! It also seemed strange that they were concerned about England's great distance from New Guinea when Jesus had specifically commanded, "Go into all the world . . ." (Mark 16:15)

But this missionary society was apparently put off by long distances. Did these brothers not believe that God would provide everything they needed? And finally: If they had wanted to get to know us better, they would have found an opportunity; of that we were convinced. The conclusion that we should accept it all as "God's decision" caused us to smile. How could people, who obviously had so little interest, so little foresight, and so little faith, put themselves in the position of knowing the will of God? For that reason, we didn't follow the advice of that mission organization and broke off all contact with them, which, I believe, suited them well.

Although so much indifference was getting to us, we decided to carry on. God's call had been too clear for us to give up.

By that time, the Lord had given us a lovely little daughter. To provide for my tiny family and make the most of the waiting time, I decided to look for work. Packing small Bible booklets, for which I received modest compensation, was not really what I had imagined missionary service to be, but it had its advantages. I was able to work at Scripture Gift Mission in a positive Christian environment, and some of the senior brothers even showed genuine interest in my plans and were willing to help me along. Ashley Baker, in particular, was determined to get me to the place where God had called me.

Mr. Baker had started small many years ago and was now the leader of the mission. He was a lovely man who could also get down to business quickly. His round, rosy face, adorned with gold-rimmed glasses, radiated warmth. When Mr. Baker learned of my request, he offered to write to a friend who was the general secretary of a missionary society in the United States. I gratefully accepted this offer, and not long afterwards a letter was on its way. We confidently expected an answer soon, but still after several weeks, nothing had come.

Mr. Baker could not accept this silence as an answer and wrote again. Once again, however, there was no response. He was so worried about these developments that he suggested I write a few lines to him, expressing my interest in the mission and attaching a short testimonial. I did this as quickly as possible and waited.

A few weeks later, I wrote again to ask why I hadn't heard anything. It was almost unbelievable, but finally we received a letter from the Regions Beyond Missionary Union (RBMU) in Philadelphia, Pennsylvania. The General Secretary of the missionary society, Mr. Vine, began his letter with apologies and explained the situation: In the first envelope he had only found my short life report, but not my letter, which would also have contained the address. Of course, he didn't know what to do with such sparse and incomplete information. After my second letter, he was able to put the pieces of the puzzle together. For a moment, it seemed as if something was finally going to get moving. For once, my age wasn't a problem either—a major hurdle seemed overcome. After filling out the application forms, we received the incredible and exciting news that we had been accepted as missionaries for New Guinea without any further delays or misunderstandings. But then another obstacle arose: Because the American office was responsible for the work in New Guinea, we were supposed to attend a preparatory course in the United States. But since they couldn't advance us the money for the passage, the matter came to a standstill again. Where should two penniless students who just finished their education and with a baby get the astronomical sum which was necessary for the crossing of the Atlantic? Fortunately, we barely had the time to get discouraged. The RBMU office in London generously offered to pay for the crossing, and Ruth's father also contributed.

Suddenly we had enough money to cover our expenses. Overjoyed, we left England and were able to enjoy a whole week of luxury on board the German passenger ship *Hanseatic*, which left Southampton on August 22, 1960. At last, we were on our way!

To our surprise, we were not greeted by gangsters and cowboys and immediately fell in love with America. Our affection for this great country has grown even more over the years. The first impressions were simply overwhelming. As we drove from New York Harbor, we were greatly impressed by the excellent road system. It was exhilarating to enter one of the gleaming clean roadside restaurants and choose from 28 different flavors of ice cream. We ordered an exotic flavor on the assumption that it would be "currently sold out." However, a smiling and friendly waitress served us what we had ordered without delay and even brought us a glass of water to go with it. But it wasn't just the waitresses who were friendly; the spontaneous warmth of the people in general was remarkable to us. Soon after we had moved into our room in the headquarters of the missionary society, we felt like the Israelites when they entered the Promised Land. We had arrived in the land where "milk and dollars flow".

The preparatory course for prospective missionaries, to which we had been invited, started immediately. It was good to get to know future colleagues and become acquainted with missionary practices. Of course, we were most fascinated by the reports on New Guinea, which gave us insights, first-hand accounts, and dozens of slides of that fascinating country. We eagerly soaked up the scent of earth and smoke that still clung to them. Perhaps we would soon be part of this mysterious life. We said a hopeful goodbye to our future missionary colleagues at the end of the course. "See you soon in New Guinea," we shouted excitedly to each other.

However, we still had to pass one exam—perhaps the most difficult of all. The course increased our motivation as well as our expectations. We were hoping to depart, however we lacked the means. It was planned that we should spend the first five years in New Guinea. That meant that we had to buy equipment and clothes for the whole time. A significant amount was necessary to cover the travel expenses, plus an additional monthly income. The mission did not have the funds for this purpose. It was assumed that we would present our request to various churches that would be willing to provide for our financial needs. However, this became a problem for us because we were strangers in this country and the communities that could help us. There were only rare invitations with an opportunity to present our request. Although we were warmly welcomed everywhere and received some financial help, it was nowhere near enough. We found ourselves at a dead end. One day after another passed without any change. As a foreigner, I couldn't count on a work permit, so my options were limited.

For months, my main responsibilities consisted of washing dishes, mowing the lawn and doing odd jobs around the mission building. This situation changed very little until December of 1960.

From December 4th to 11th, 1960, the Congress for World Missions took place at the Moody Church in Chicago, Illinois. Mission leaders and missionaries from all over the world came together to discuss mission strategies and hear reports from various mission fields. Mr. Vine also wanted to attend and kindly invited me to accompany him. I gratefully accepted, although I didn't see much point in attending, as the congress was for missionaries, not for those who wanted to become missionaries. What could missionaries and mission leaders, who needed financial support themselves, do for me? At best, I still had the prospect of learning more about missionary service in general. Besides, it was a good change from the boring duties at the mission home.

When I arrived at the congress, I felt out of place among the men and women who had proven themselves on mission fields all over the world. All of them were very friendly, but whenever someone tried to start a conversation with me, I flinched a little. Everyone who saw my name tag asked me: "How long have you been in New Guinea?" It didn't sound spiritual at all when I had to say: "I haven't even been there yet."

Then the lectures began. Without exception, the missionaries reported that they lacked workers for their mission field. Their appeals were extremely urgent: "Where are the young people who are willing to go on missions?"

Mission songs were sung in between. "Who is on God's side? Who is ready to serve the King?" rang out across the congregation. I sat in my row and cried. *"Don't you hear me, God? Don't you want to finally do something?"*

After a particularly moving message, I went to the front and met the head of a well-known Bible school, to whom I told my woes. Unfortunately, he was too busy. With a fatherly gesture, he put his hand on my shoulder and prayed: "Father, let him keep at it."

No doubt the good man thought he had behaved appropriately for the situation. The congress continued, and other calls followed. "What about your Christian commitment?" the speakers appealed to the audience. "We are on the side of the Lord, we want to serve the King," came the prompt reply.

As the last day of the conference approached, I was dejected and, above all, angry. Angry at God, because he had not kept his end of the bargain. He had let me down. In a fit of childish rage, I told him how I felt.

"*Look, Lord,*" I began with enormous self-righteousness. "*I gave up my job, I left my home country, I completed several years of training, and all that because I wanted to serve you! If, however, you are not at all interested in my service, then that's fine with me. Then I will not be a missionary and depart for the Netherlands tomorrow. If you don't make a move today, then it's all over.*"

I was dead serious and was convinced that I would be preparing to travel home to the Netherlands the next day.

The last item on the conference agenda that evening was a church service. I went and determined not to give God the slightest chance. I deliberately arrived too early and went to the front row, which usually remained empty. As I sat down, I liked the thought that no one would be sitting next to me. Hadn't I promised the Lord that I wouldn't be the least bit in his way?

That evening, people flocked to the church in droves. Even the front rows, including the seats next to me, were soon filled.

The service was not much different from the previous ones, except that the missionaries' pleas for more workers seemed more urgent than ever. Then came the end, the last call, the last verse of the gathered congregation. No, the speaker still had an announcement to make: "Before you go home, it would be nice if you would shake hands with the person sitting next to you and briefly introduce yourself." That was typically American. I didn't feel like it, because what could I say? My career as a missionary was over before it had really begun. I wanted to start my journey home the next day. Without much enthusiasm, I turned to the man on my right, who had already stood up to greet me.

"Teeuwen," I introduced myself. "Jacques Teeuwen." He replied in a friendly manner: "My name is David Marshall, and I am Pastor of Grace Church in Ridgewood, New Jersey."

Then he frowned thoughtfully. "Jacques Teeuwen," he said, "where have I heard that name before?"

At that moment, I realized that God was at work and Satan's stronghold was beginning to crumble.

After the conference, I packed my suitcases in a daze. The time had come to leave, but not for the Netherlands! It was incomprehensible to me, but the almighty God had graciously given me an answer, even though I had literally blackmailed him. Once again, he had revealed his unfathomable goodness.

As it turned out, Grace Church had heard about us through RBMU. Somehow, however, the connection between us was broken, apparently because several letters back and forth went missing. Grace Church had never received an answer to their request to get more information about us.

But now, Pastor Marshall and I confronted each other at the end of the last mission conference which I had planned to attend. We talked briefly about theological questions, but then about finances. I told him that we needed at least 1,200 dollars for the crossing to New Guinea, then another 170 dollars a month for our personal needs and money for equipment for the next five years. That was a lot of money at the time, but little did we know about God's abundant generosity.

To my surprise, Pastor Marshall didn't say "no" right away, but he couldn't make any promises either, except that we would hear from him. A few weeks later, Ruth and I were invited to the annual Grace Church missions conference. We almost missed each other again, as Pastor Marshall was waiting at one bus station in Ridgewood while we got off at another. However, we finally found each other in time for the evening event, which was an unforgettable experience for us. Once we arrived, our fears began to melt away like snow in summer, as we were welcomed with warmth and great sympathy, making us feel right at home. There was no attempt to trap us, nor were there any petty theological disputes or personal convictions, but the focus was on the cause itself. After the weekend, we felt spiritually strengthened and encouraged that one day we would get to New Guinea after all.

A few days later, the phone rang at the mission house. Pastor Marshall was on the phone. What he told us was almost unbelievable: "The Grace Church voted unanimously to pay the entire cost."

I was about to burst into loud cheers, but then Pastor Marshall suddenly said: "We only have one condition." The thought immediately struck me that this would be something I certainly couldn't do, because it had always been like this before. It was probably over. My heart pounding, I expected the worst.

The Teeuwen family before going out as missionaries—Ruth, Priscilla, and Jacques

"The condition is that you don't delay with further studies but set off for New Guinea as soon as possible." Relieved, I shouted my agreement into the telephone receiver. This was what we wanted! Together with Ruth and little Priscilla, we danced around the house. An unbelievable thing had happened! God's call had reached me in Wiedenest more than five years ago, and now all the signals were green lights. With renewed energy,

I devoted myself to washing up and mowing the lawn, because the end was already in sight. An exciting few weeks followed. Since we had arrived in the USA, we had always had some free time to ourselves, but that was about to change. We had to take care of the necessary vaccinations and pack boxes. We had to buy clothes, shoes and household items for the whole family for the next few years. Who would predict that our family would still only consist of three people? Should we take only girls' clothes with us, or perhaps also things for a little boy?

The sizes of the clothes were a chapter in themselves. One church surprised us by generously donating all of Priscilla's needs for the next five years. Loyal friends then transported the packed goods to New York Harbor.

The big day arrived on July 21st, 1961. Our little family boarded the passenger ship *Medon* of the Royal Dutch Steamship Company. The first stop was Curaçao, where we docked on July 26th. From there we were to transfer to the *Roepat*, which came from Amsterdam and was due to set sail for Hollandia,[1] the then capital of Irian Jaya, on July 29th.

In Curaçao, we learned that the *Roepat* was delayed. The departure date was postponed several times, but finally we were able to leave Curaçao on August 12th. As Hollandia still seemed so far away, this delay didn't bother us much; I was only worried about the extra costs that would be incurred as the result of this delay. We spent one night at the San Marco Hotel in Willemstad. The next day, a fellow traveler who had accompanied us from New York and lived in Curaçao came to say goodbye. When he heard about our dilemma, he offered us his beach house to stay in; we even had a car and a boat at our disposal, and all that free of charge! So, we spent the next few days swimming and fishing and recharging our batteries in the tropical sun. We almost regretted it when the *Roepat* finally turned up.

Again, we had many reasons to be thankful to God, who had given us this generous friend and the unexpected vacation.

The trip on the *Roepat* was also an unforgettable experience. For weeks we were surrounded only by blue sky and water. The immeasurable vastness of the ocean left a deep impression on us. The changing play of bright

---

[1] Capital on the north coast of West New Guinea. Known as Jayapura since 1968.

colors and light effects made us newly aware of the creator and sustainer. Every now and then a school of flying fish broke the surface of the water and silvery, streamlined bodies soared upwards as the waves rolled up and down tirelessly.

After eleven days, we saw the blue, mysterious mountains of Tahiti rising out of the water. As soon as the ship had docked, we were already on our way to explore the beauty of this magnificent island, which was hardly visited by tourists at the time. The tranquil pace of life there captivated us as much as the pleasant temperatures and lush tropical vegetation. We were fascinated by the giant coconut palms, banana trees, hibiscus flowers, and the red and purple bougainvillea entwined around white-painted houses.

We learned from the locals that a flower, called "frangi-pani," exudes a beguiling exotic fragrance all day long if you wear it behind your ear. We also discovered an ancient statue of Kon-tiki on the island and thought about the consequences of Captain Cook's landing on the island in 1797. A plaque with a Bible verse[2] in three languages commemorated this event. We were slightly saddened when, after three days, it was time to continue our journey. The piercing honking of the *Roepat* called us back.

As we left the harbor, we took off our wreaths of flowers—following the advice of friends—and threw them overboard. According to tradition, if the wreaths washed back to shore, it meant that one day we would return to Tahiti. We hoped that they would not drift out to sea. Was it any wonder that we fell under the spell of this island so quickly?

But the comfortable life couldn't go on like this forever. Further stops were the Solomon Islands and New Caledonia, and we were getting closer and closer to our destination.

Our attitude also began to change. At the beginning of the journey, we had been captivated by the vastness and timelessness of the ocean and wished that this carefree life would go on forever. Now we were starting to get impatient when we thought about what awaited us in New Guinea. And, of course, we were also a little scared. The freighter

---

2   John 3:16: "For God so loved the world that he gave his one and only Son, that whoever believes in him shall not perish but have eternal life."

had been our home for the last few weeks—the rhythmic pounding of the engines had become as familiar as our heartbeat. We felt free of responsibility and, on the one hand, wanted this to last forever. At the same time, we were aware that it couldn't be like that and couldn't make us happy in the long term. Soon our lives would look completely different. Our little family felt safe on board the ship. And a little bit of security would have been reassuring for a family with a two-year-old daughter and a wife who was six months pregnant.

INTO THE STONE AGE

ARLY IN the morning I left our comfortable cabin on board the Dutch freighter *Roepat* and went up on deck to stretch my legs and get a breath of fresh, salty sea-air. I knew we were getting close to our destination, but when suddenly I saw the contours of New Guinea's[1] mountains emerging from the distant waters, I panicked.

After five years of uncertainty while making arrangements to go to the mission field, we had sailed on July 21, 1961. Now we were about to meet our calling.

The dark, jagged peaks looming ahead pierced whatever bubbly dreams I had been entertaining about our destiny, revealing in all its fullness the challenge before us. How did I get here in the first place? What on earth had made me decide to come? *"Lord, I'll do anything and go anywhere,"* my own words re-echoed in my mind. I had made this commitment alone and in all sincerity. Later on I had begun to tell others about my intentions, sometimes because was necessary, and at other times even though it was

---

1 New Guinea—Indonesia, a former Dutch colony, gained independence in 1948, with the exception of New Guinea, which did not become an Indonesian province until 1963. It has been known under a variety of names, including Dutch New Guinea, West Irian, and Irian Jaya. Today it is the Indonesian province of Papua.

quite unnecessary—admiring glances in my direction, words of appreciation, and promises of intercession had gone to my head. Full of the things I was expecting to achieve, I had, in my own mind, already become an accomplished missionary hero—rather like a boy who pages through a booklet on aircraft and begins to see himself as a fully trained jumbo-jet pilot.

To dream is a good start. But the accomplishment of noble intentions requires hard work and sacrifice. Now the dreaming was over. Supporters had disappeared. The stage was empty for me. Reality had to be faced: danger, dirt, loneliness, a primitive lifestyle. I just did not have what it would take.

"Lord, what am I going to do?" I cried suddenly. *"I cannot go back now. What will people say? I can't be a failure before I've even started. But neither can I handle what lies ahead. Lord, what am I going to do? Where are You?"*

He was right there. A very present help in trouble (Psalm 46:1). A presence much more reassuring than the safe, rhythmic throbbing of the freighter-engines or the well-meaning words of any supporter.

He gave me these words:

"The Lord is my light and my salvation; whom shall I fear?" (Psalm 27:1).

A good question. Whom indeed?

It was all I needed.

Mary Widbin was waiting to welcome Ruth, myself, and our little Priscilla on arrival at the quay in Hollandia. Having already spent four years on the field she seemed a very senior missionary to us. She was cheerful and happy. Her attitude gave me confidence to fire the first of many questions to her.

"Is our house ready yet?" We had been told that our colleagues, in anticipation of our coming, would build a house for us. We in turn would help to build for the people arriving after us.

Mary giggled.

"They haven't even started yet. You'll have to do it yourself."

She seemed to think it was a big joke.

"All I've ever built is a simple bookcase," I stammered.

"By the time you've finished your house, you'll be a qualified carpenter," Mary laughed.

She put the VW-Kombi in gear and with a jerk we set off towards our temporary home on the mission compound on the coast. When we entered the door of the boiling hot aluminium structure a fat rat scuffled away, disappearing down the open drain of the doorless bathroom.

I hadn't realized I would need Psalm 27:1 so soon.

Immigration formalities were taken care of within days. October 6, 1961, was the red-letter day when we boarded a Missionary Aviation Fellowship[1] Cessna 180 for the small settlement of Karubaga, some 150 miles inland, as our destination. Our pilot was a charming lady named Betty Greene.

We flew over swamps, jungles, foothills, and mountains. Then, suddenly, we were back in the Stone Age. As our plane descended into the Swart Valley, we were anxious to see and take in as much as possible. The little round huts with their grass-covered roofs through which blue smoke ascended almost looked familiar, after all the slides and photographs we had poured over. As the plane made its final approach I saw a dark brown man, almost naked, leap towards the landing area. Then we touched down and taxied over the bumpy grass strip towards the parking space.

---

1 Mission Aviation Fellowship – a missionary society that provides trained pilots and aircraft to serve other missions.

The few familiar faces of missionaries seemed to submerge in a sea of brown bodies and inquisitive faces which surged forward as soon as the propeller stopped turning. Someone opened the door. Out of the hubbub and bustle around the aircraft words of our new language began to crystallize, as uninhibited men and women called out their greetings.

"Wa, nore. Wa!"[1] "Welcome my friend. Welcome!"

Priscilla, who had celebrated her second birthday on board the *Roepat*, had been sitting on my lap during the one hour and fifty minutes flight. She was the first to evaluate our new friends. "Daddy," she called in disgust, "they've all got dirty noses!" She wrinkled her own little snub-nose in disdain. Her observation was only too correct. People without clothes don't have handkerchiefs. However, there was undoubtedly more to be discovered than that. We disembarked in order to find out for ourselves.

---

[1] Orthography—Dani was an unwritten language until the arrival of missionaries. It was at first written phonetically. International participation of missions resulted in a variety of spellings. Later, when the New Testament was translated, qualified linguists determined set rules for spelling. Dani language written in this book still represents the original attempts.

THE LAND FORGOTTEN BY GOD

MISSIONARIES HAVE been working in New Guinea for several hundred years. In established coastal areas, doctrinally sound churches could be found. The Christian message of salvation, however, had not yet penetrated the dense jungle areas of the interior. Parts of the gospel reached inland from the coast, but the message was always twisted in some way, like the following account of creation:

> God was very busy. Time had passed faster than expected. Suddenly it was already Saturday evening. Sunday would soon be upon us, and then there would be no more work to do. Hadn't he himself designated Sunday as a day of rest? God looked around benevolently. He had really enjoyed the past week. He had decided to create a world and simply started designing things. The results were so fascinating that his enthusiasm had run away with him.
>
> What God had created was much more than what was necessary. Much of what he had brought into being was already in the right place. But a lot of artistic creations remained. The works of his hands were scattered untidily throughout the heavenly

realms. In view of this, a day of rest seemed highly inappropriate. What should he do with what was left?

Then God had an idea and his face brightened. Determined to get his affairs in order before Sunday, God scoured the heavens and gathered the surplus things of his creation as he found them: a mighty mountain range where the peaks were bare and rugged and the valleys deeply carved; a few hills covered with grass and bushes; a wild, torrential river and then a few acres of jungle forest with majestic towering trees, swampy lowlands, a myriad of magnificent, brightly colored birds, slimy, slippery snakes, cunning crocodiles and countless smaller animals. Finally, there was a melodiously murmuring stream over there that also needed a place. When God could be sure that nothing else was lying around, he grabbed the whole colorful assortment of landscapes and creatures and hurled them into space with a single sweep of his mighty arm. According to this legend, this is how New Guinea appeared on the globe. The land that God

The land that God created on Saturday night.

created on Saturday night. Only now could the seventh day really be a day of rest.

Even these vague and twisted fragments of the biblical message were lost before they could reach over the mighty mountain ranges. Behind them, the word of God did not exist, and the name "Jesus" had never been heard. "The land forgotten by God" therefore seemed an appropriate name. It was no wonder really that the Gospel had never been preached here. Until 1945, less than two decades prior to our arrival, nobody had known that these remote mountains were populated.

Towards the end of World War II, a US airplane was reported missing over the New Guinea territory. The ensuing search brought results that were beyond imagination. In the Central Highlands, approximately where the muddy, slow Baliem River cut its way towards the lowlands in the North, large concentrations of a pigmy-type people were discovered. It seemed incredible that these tribes could have been living here with the world-at-large totally unaware of their existence.

To some people however, the discovery meant a challenge. The Church of Jesus Christ sprang to attention at the news. Here was one of the bigger spiritual challenges of the twentieth century. Here were people who had never heard the name of Jesus Christ. Thousands of unreached people, living and dying in sin, unaware of the way of escape He had provided.

For many praying people all over the world, missionary songs like this gained a new meaning:

> To the regions beyond I must go, I must go,
> Where the story has never been told.
> To the millions that never have heard of His love
> I must tell the sweet story of old[1]

In 1954 the Christian and Missionary Alliance sent its first workers into the Baliem Valley. Other evangelical missions moved into adjacent areas. In 1955 an amphibious mission plane landed on Lake Archbold, several

---

1 Albert B. Simpson (1904)

days trekking towards the North. From there missionary pioneers moved west towards Bokondini, where an airstrip was constructed.

In May 1956, RBMU (Regions Beyond Missionary Union) missionaries Bill Widbin and Paul Geshwein left Bokondini and trekked southwest into the Swart Valley, which they had first surveyed from the air. In April 1957 they returned to the Swart Valley and started building an airstrip in Karubaga. The first landing was made on June 7, 1957. In August 1960, Kanggyme was opened, followed by Mamit on April 21, 1961. These three stations were located in the Swart Valley—where we were to spend the next thirteen years of our lives.

This area, behind the lofty mountain ranges of Central New Guinea, was where we had just touched down in the little Cessna airplane.

DIRTY NOSES AND DIRTY NEEDLES

AFTER A few days in Karubaga our little family was flown to Kanggyme, where John and Helen Dekker were holding the fort. We moved into a small shed which they had previously used as a storeroom. Our household goods had not yet arrived. We borrowed what was needed from the Dekkers. Sleeping was a bit of a problem (it was not cold), but Ruth, who was expecting our second child, felt very uncomfortable sleeping on a thin piece of foam rubber. But there was no alternative: our mattresses were yet to be flown in. We cooked on a wood stove. There were no indoor facilities. There was no running water.

"*Niyo torinak,*" I said expectantly to the stocky fellow standing in front of me. His big brown eyes looked at me questioningly. I walked over to the wordlist which was pricked into the bark wall. I had used the right phrase. Carefully articulating, I slowly repeated the sentence.

"*Ni-yo to-ri-nak.*"

Somewhat embarrassed, my helper pointed apologetically at his ears. "*Naruk konenggeelik o, nore.*" I would have understood him without the little gesture. That phrase was the usual response to my attempts at speaking the Dani language of the Swart Valley. "I don't understand, my friend."

I picked up a bucket and pointed towards the spring.

We moved into a small shed previously used as a storeroom.

"*Ai, nore.*" A look of understanding swept over the boy's face. "*Ai, nore. Niyo torinakit, kagi o,*" he responded, slurring the syllables into what seemed only one word. Taking the bucket, he leaped outside and bounded towards the spring, whooping excitedly as he went. His bare brown body glistened in the morning sun. I mumbled the magic words again, still not sure why my rendition had been incomprehensible.

We were blessed to have that wordlist. It consisted of only one sheet, but every expression written on it was useful:

> Come — *mok o*
> light the fire — *kany kunimok*
> draw water — *niyo torinak*
> I don't understand — *naruk konenggeelik o*
> thank you, my friend — *wa, nore*
> go away — *nak o*

Especially the last phrase we used frequently! *Nak o*—go away!

It seemed the only defence available against being followed around continually by inquisitive natives. They tagged along behind us when we were outside, and peered through numerous cracks in the walls when we were inside our little home.

Our pleas for privacy did not avail. Before the sun rose, dozens of noisy and filthy people would gather outside our house. They would stand on their toes and crane their necks to catch a glimpse of what was going on inside whenever the door was opened. The stench of unwashed bodies would waft in. Flies, busily occupied on festering, unattended sores, would quickly change location and land on us—and our food!

"*Nanip, nanip,*" we would cajole and plead, using the plural form of *nak*. But we might as well have addressed the surrounding mountains. Our words didn't cause a stir.

We couldn't really blame the Danis. After all, who had ever seen anything quite as incredible as these strange white beings who had taken up residence in Kanggyme?

Going outside was even more of an ordeal. As soon as we took one ste out of our doors, people would come running to join those already at the doorstep. Everybody clamoured for attention. Once a man simply planted his feet firmly in front of us, blocking our path.

"I will bring you firewood," he shouted, the offer sounding more like an order. We were only expected to nod consent.

Dirty fingernails would scratch our bare arms to gain our attention. A mother holding a sick baby pointed at the little one's dirt-caked buttocks and yelled above the din, "Needle! Needle!"

A young fellow felt fully confident that he, above all the others, understood the ways of these newcomers. He knew they did not like dirty noses. So, wiping his filthy nose with both hands and then rubbing them together, he enquired pleasantly, "Shall I pick strawberries for you?" (He was rather surprised when we declined his kind offer.)

It was tempting to stay indoors all day. But we simply had to mingle with the people. They were the reason for everything we had worked at in the past few years.

In some ways, these people seemed so degraded that we yearned for a transformation in their lives.

Most people were covered with yaws, tropical sores that ate away their bodies. Every day we made our way to the clinic, a primitive shed with a grass-covered roof and a dirt floor. Day after day patients would throng outside, waiting impatiently for their turn to be treated.[1]

"*Liiru! Liiru!*" they would shout, pointing at their buttocks, as if we could not see and imagine that they had come for a "needle."

One man refused to turn around. He had a sore on his face, so why should I inject a needle in his bottom?

A woman came with two babies. One was covered with sores, the other was perfectly healthy. The mother insisted that both receive a *liiru*. After all, they were twins.

While the bedlam continued, a pan of water would stand on a burning Primus stove atop the rough wooden counter in the clinic. After having been used a dozen times, each of the few needles we possessed would be dropped in the boiling water for a while. That was the only available

Jacques extracting a tooth

---

1   Yaws, or framboise, (both words mean raspberry) is a skin disease with sores resembling raspberries. With penicillin treatment, this disease gradually disappeared.

method of sterilization. It was also the only way in which we could begin to meet the demands of the impatient, disorderly, and demanding crowd at the door.

As if by a miracle, the treatment was successful. Quite soon the yaws began to disappear. Teeth were extracted, babies were delivered, arrow wounds were treated, lives were saved. Even though not everybody received the much desired *liiru*-treatment, our medical aid made a definite impact upon the people.

A GIFT FOR PRISCILLA

I REMEMBER AN incident about a week after our arrival in Kanggyme. A group of men had gathered in front of our hut; all seemed calm and cheerful. Jipagan—a strong, muscular man—led the group. Flashing his large teeth, he pointed at a piglet, repeatedly pronouncing the name *patilak*. We wondered what he was trying to tell us and made it clear that we were not interested in buying a pig. However, the men were not deterred; they patiently remained seated and waited. Baffled, we asked John Dekker for advice. As he listened to the men's explanations, he struggled to hide a laugh, which was understandable when we were told what the men wanted.

"They want to give you this pig," John chuckled, "for free, without payment." We felt flattered. Wasn't that really a sign of a friendly bond? Our self-esteem increased enormously. But why was John still giggling?

"In reality, they want to give the pig to your Priscilla," John continued. Only now did we begin to understand. "Patilak" was the Dani's name for Priscilla. But why Priscilla should be given this privilege was not yet clear to us. At last John came out with the explanation. "Priscilla is to receive it as a dowry," John said, trying in vain to remain serious. "That's why they're not asking for payment." Priscilla was just two years old!

It was not uncommon among the Dani for a girl to be sold at birth to an older man by money-hungry relatives. A down payment equivalent to a few pigs was enough to make the deal legally binding. As soon as the girl showed signs of physical maturity, the buyer claimed his property and a final agreement was made.

"Why don't you just accept the gift?" John suggested. After a brief exchange of words, the pig was handed over to me. John made his way home to continue his language studies. About an hour later, I realized to my surprise that the men were still there. When they were still sitting in the same place two hours later, I decided to consult John again.

"Maybe you could give them a small steel axe," he said, "That will show them that you recognize their gift." I don't think any of the men understood a word I said to them. The steel axe spoke a clearer language. Overjoyed, they took it and were gone within minutes. A steel axe was roughly the equivalent of a pig of that size.

FEAR

Once an obnoxious fellow jumped the queue at the clinic. He seemed convinced of his own importance. All I saw was a dirty old man, decorated with a pig tusk through his nose, an ostrich feather sticking out of the net bag covering his hair, and bracelets of cowrie shells around his arms. When he insisted on coming inside instead of waiting outside the door like everyone else, I forcibly ejected him. The man turned out to be a chief. He neither argued nor resisted, but simply walked off.

This unusual reaction caused me to feel uneasy. What would he do? He was not the only one to react to me in this way. No quarrel, no fight, just a flickering in the eye and off they would go.

Why? I couldn't match this behaviour with the violent and aggressive attitudes the Danis displayed amongst themselves. Did it have something to do with their custom of killing strangers who visited their valley? Was I a marked man? Were they simply waiting for a suitable occasion? I became frightened.

One night I was lying in bed and, as usual, unable to sleep. The tiny bedroom was pitch dark. My eyes sought in vain to pierce the smothering blackness: I could barely see where the bark wall ceased and the small plastic windows began. If only there could have been a streetlight outside! But in this deep, hidden valley, surrounded by bleak mountains, there was nothing that even resembled a light. No moon or stars were visible above, only a heavy overcast. The house was full of eerie noises. The aluminium roof, cooling down in the gentle night breeze, squeaked as it shrunk back to size. The wooden structure moaned and groaned. When the dog so much as stirred under the house, I cringed, certain that he would start barking in alarm. My heart throbbed in my throat as I lay there. I was desperately afraid. In the thick darkness it would be impossible to detect the outline of a dark body. Would they come for me tonight? Were they now ready to take revenge for the rude way in which I had sometimes treated them? Our limited understanding of the language had caused additional tension.

Sometimes I was really afraid of them

Quite apart from the fear of death, there was the worry gnawing at my insides that I would soon collapse under the pressure of it all. If I could not overcome this fear, my missionary days were numbered. I would be a failure: destroyed by fear at the outset of the battle.

The situation became more and more difficult when John and Helen had to leave Kanggyme temporarily. Ruth, Priscilla and I were the only white people remaining in the area. Our nearest colleagues lived in Karubaga, some twenty-five kilometers away. Only a narrow, hazardous mountain trail connected the two stations. Otherwise, Karubaga could only be reached by plane—in the daytime, and if the weather permitted. I could draw little comfort from the literal meaning of the name of our station: Kanggyme, "place of death."

Throughout the hours of the night, I would keep reminding myself that the Danis would plan any attack shortly before dawn, as they were afraid of the dark themselves. So each night I lay awake, waiting anxiously for the expected pre-dawn attack.

How I longed for the morning to come! In bright daylight everything looked so different. My fears would evaporate like the early morning mists that covered the mountains. During the daytime life had to continue as usual.

As a family, we were in the habit of having a time of reading and prayer after every meal. Wednesday nights were different. After tucking Priscilla under the blankets, Ruth and I would have a prayer meeting and Bible study—one of those strange customs we had brought along with us from across the oceans. In the absence of a teacher, we would often listen to a cassette-tape recording. One particular Wednesday evening, the speaker dropped a comment about *the bondage of fear* (Romans 8:15). That phrase stuck. There I was, a born-again Christian, fully persuaded that I had been *made free in the Son* (John 8:36), yet at the same time plagued by a dreadful fear. And the Bible referred to it as bondage.

For the next few nights I had something to think about as I lay awake and listened for suspicious sounds. Finally I came round to committing my case to the Lord. I told Him I was scared. I asked Him to deliver me. And that is precisely what He did, right there and then! It was absolutely undramatic and unemotional, but my fear vanished completely. Did I ever sleep that night! God had done a total and wonderful work in me, without which I would never have been able to face the trials still ahead.

NABELAN KABELAN

THE MEDICAL work was only one way in which we gained the confidence of the people. Other ways were our apparent supernatural powers and alleged connections with the spirit-world. Had not a great bird of steel without so much as a flap of its wings delivered us from the skies where the spirits presided? Before our appearance among the tribal people, they had gazed at our mission planes as they flew over on survey flights. It was soon determined that these aircraft were evil spirits responsible for the high rate of infant mortality. Seeing that we had appeared from out of the belly of one of these monsters, the Danis assumed that we held sway over life and death. Our incredible achievements with the *liiru* only strengthened this belief.

And then there were the frequent conversations we had with our ancestors in the sky. Many of the people had heard with their own ears, as every morning at 7 o'clock we switched on our transmitter-receiver and reported to the coastal mission base or had "traffic" for and from other stations. The voices of our deceased fathers would boom forth from the little magic box, informing us whether another steel bird would be arriving that day, what the weather was going to be like and what was happening in surrounding areas. Uncannily, our ancestors were usually right.

Long after the majority of natives had become Christians and had given up the idea that our "Missavia" was indwelt by spirits, they kept insisting that the radio knew everything. One day three years later, a fine Christian man came to see me. He was a quiet, pleasant sort of fellow, who, unlike many of his fellow-tribesmen, had never demanded much attention. But now he had a problem.

After the usual greetings, he explained, "Some time ago you gave me a steel knife. Somehow I've mislaid it. I have looked everywhere, but cannot find it..." He then requested politely, "Could you please ask your radio where it is?" (I was sorry to have to let him down. As he walked away, I could see that he was disappointed, too. Why was I unwilling to help when all I had to do was turn the switch and pop the question for him?)

We were very much aware that in order to deliver the spiritual message entrusted to us, we needed to do more than simply impress the people with technology and medical aid. But what could we do? We were still struggling for mastery over basic grammar and vocabulary of the complicated Dani language, so how could we possibly convey such concepts as forgiveness, peace, reconciliation—to mention only a few? Not only did we still have to find correct Dani words for these concepts, but we were also still searching for a key, any key, to enter into the spiritual understanding of the people.

The Scriptures encouraged us to keep searching and learning. Jesus, who had given us the command, "Go ye," had also provided us with His promise, "I am with you." (Matthew 28:19-20) And if the apostle Peter told us to follow in Christ's steps, we could only conclude that He had gone on before us. He was there ahead of us, to prepare the way for His Kingdom and to solve our problems in proclaiming it.

That is *precisely* how things turned out. Missionaries who had entered neighbouring valleys prior to our arrival, had discovered among the Dani people a deep longing for something they called "Nabelan Kabelan." It soon became clear that here was a God-given key for the opening of the hearts of the Dani population. The missionaries, once they understood, had a simple message to deliver: "Jesus Christ has the secret of Nabelan Kabelan." The response in these neighbouring valleys, where mission work had gone on a little longer than in our Swart Valley, had been instantaneous. "Who is this Jesus Christ? What does He want us to do?"

Missionaries from these areas soon came to our valley, repeating the message to our people. They brought along some of their native converts who eagerly confirmed the message. "Jesus Christ has the secret of Nabelan Kabelan." Although the Danis of the Swart Valley had previously had little or no contact with these fellow-tribespeople from surrounding valleys, they, too, responded with overwhelming enthusiasm. "Who is Jesus? What does He want us to do?"

And so the news about Nabelan Kabelan swept through the valleys.

So what is Nabelan Kabelan? There are various versions, but this is how, after a number of years, the story was told to me.

With a dozen or so men, we were sitting on the mud floor of a Dani hut. Some men were leaning comfortably against the walls of rough hand-hewn timber. Others sat around the small fire in the centre of the hut. The flames danced and crackled, as the pungent smells of smoke and bodies filled the air. Several men were conversing in low, murmuring voices. Outside, the rain was pelting down. Through the door opening other huts were visible, blue rings of smoke rising slowly from their pointed grass roofs.

I was quite accustomed to sitting with the people like this. Kindly, someone would always offer me a leaf, a rock, or a piece of board to sit on. As sat there that evening, I said to the men next to me, "Tell me again about Nabelan Kabelan." Faces lit up as quickly as conversations died down. The Danis loved to tell stories and reminisce.

Someone cleared his throat.

"An yikit-e?" a young fellow suggested. "Shall I say it?" *"Yooru,"* the others agreed. "You say it."

Though he was only a teenager, his face had already been disfigured by warfare. An arrow had destroyed one of his eyes. But his healthy eye sparkled happily. He cleared his throat and began.

"Men . . ." They always did that. Every story, every report started with this three-letter word. It gave the speaker a final brief opportunity to formulate his thoughts as the audience fell silent. "Men . . . Nabelan

112 THE SECRET OF NABELAN KABELAN

Kabelan *wone ji aret*. This is the story of Nabelan Kabelan. Our people have always been great fighters. . . ." Some of the old men in the hut murmured approval of this introduction. A younger fellow snickered at the memory of a recent fighting experience.

"Men . . . Because of the fighting many men were injured and died. So many men died that there were hardly enough left to build new gardens and gather firewood."

I could not help but glance at some of the luckier warriors sitting around me. Some of them had severely scarred bodies. I had often helped to remove broken-off arrowheads from the bodies of others.

"Men . . . Not only the men died. Many women died in childbirth."

I knew what he was talking about. I was appalled when once a couple of strapping fellows took a woman whose time had come, lifted her up and gave her a good shake to hasten delivery! Occasionally, I had helped to deliver babies under most unhygienic conditions. At first I had been somewhat embarrassed when happy young mothers pointed at me and exclaimed proudly to everyone who wanted to hear, "This is his baby."

"Men . . . Many, very many, babies died at birth. Of those who survived, many died when they were still quite small."

Right again. Cremating a stillborn baby together with the placenta just outside the hut was almost a matter of routine. Children weren't even given a name until several months old: frequently it wasn't worth the trouble because they didn't survive that long.

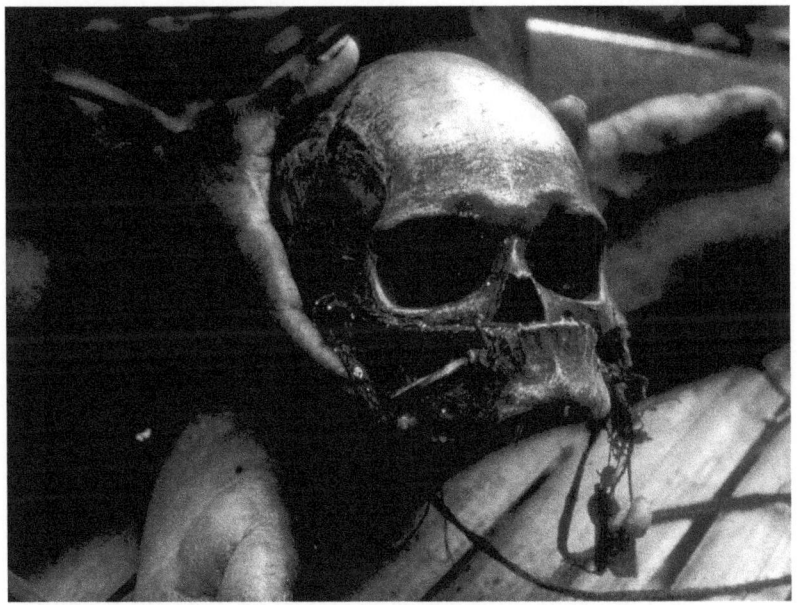

"Men . . . There was so much sickness."

A pneumonic cough of one of the older men emphasized this statement.

"So we looked for a way of escape. We were afraid of death. We were tired of it. We did not want to die, but to live forever."

There it was: the magic word. To live for ever, to obtain "Nabelan Kabelan." Eternal life!!

"Men . . . We did not know how to obtain Nabelan Kabelan. Our forefathers had told us that the snake possessed the secret of eternal life. After all, did they not find empty snakeskins from time to time?

Was this not evidence enough that the snake could die and come to life again in a new body? There was only one problem."

Nigitwariyak, the storyteller, paused for a moment. He seemed reluctant to continue until the older men, captivated by his account, urged him to.

"Men . . . The problem was how to obtain the secret from the snake. We waited and waited and waited. But the snake never came."

The faces in the audience, totally caught up in this well-known yet fascinating story, suddenly reflected something of the agony their people had gone through as they waited and hoped for the snake to come. But the snake never came.

Nigitwariyak continued. "Our fathers, who kept having to face death, began to look for reasons why the snake was unwilling to share the secret of Nabelan Kabelan. They found out that the snake was very shy. The snake did not often come close to the huts, did it? And out in the jungle it would always slither away quickly as soon as it heard people approaching. But this shyness was not the only problem. Somehow our fathers thought that the snake was also afraid of the *pirigobit*."

No further explanation was needed for those in the hut. Pirigobit was a little black and white bird, about the same size and about as common as the sparrow.

"Pirigobit, with its constant twittering, frightened the snake and prevented it from sharing the secret of Nabelan Kabelan. We tried to kill as many pirigobit as possible, but there were always many more left."

"*E-o,*" someone interrupted. "I used to kill many myself. Whenever I caught one, I would force open its beak and ram a stick down its throat so it would never, never twitter again." Almost apologetically he added, "Because we did not know, we used to do these things."

Nigitwariyak waited patiently till the older man had ceased to speak before picking up the thread of the story again.

"Men . . . The snake never came to share the secret of Nabelan Kabelan. But," here the story teller turned to me, "you white people came and after you learned our language, you told us that Jesus holds the secret of eternal life. And you came because He wanted to give it to us. What would have become of us if you had not come to tell us?"

And so it happened. Initially, superstition, fear, and confusion held sway over many of the inhabitants of the Swart Valley. But soon the conviction that Jesus Christ truly holds the secret of Nabelan Kabelan opened the door to the preaching of the Gospel in the entire valley. Once we ourselves and the people recognized the link between their search and our good news, the name of Jesus Christ spread like wildfire.

This was the situation in which we found ourselves when we first arrived. The Swart Valley had a population of some 25,000 at the time. We spent our first six months at the Kanggyme mission station. The mission field conference then re-allocated us to the Mamit station, where we moved on April 26, 1962.

Until then, Frank and Betty Clarke from Australia had been the only couple there. For more than two years they stood up courageously against the hardships and loneliness of an isolated station.

Having spent time on each of these two stations, we were personally involved as the Danis began to emerge from darkness into the marvellous light of Nabelan Kabelan. In many ways, we witnessed a perfect replay of the life and experiences of the first church as recorded in Acts 2:37-47.

FLAMES OF LOVE

THE SERVICE was a far cry from those held at Grace Church in Ridgewood, New Jersey, our sending church. How I had loved being there. The colonial-style building with its pointed black spire which was floodlit at night always looked so inviting. Entering through the wide-open, white doors did not in any way diminish one's sense of welcome and anticipation. At the entrance were smiling ushers handing out neatly printed church bulletins. Rich, red carpets led to immaculate, cream-coloured pews, where red hymnbooks with golden imprint and registration forms lay waiting. Quiet organ music prior to the service encouraged silent meditation. And with Pastor Dave Marshall in the pulpit, a gracious, soul-stirring sermon was guaranteed.

A sharp sting in my right arm jolted me out of my reveries. Instinctively I slapped my arm, killing the insect which had caused the pain. I was back in the Dani service. Several hundred people sat on the ground around me. Their sweaty faces glistened in the hot sunlight. Babies were crying. Young children were engrossed in delousing each other. These services, usually continuing for hours on end, were quite an ordeal. The odour of unwashed, perspiring bodies hung over the crowd like a heavy, suffocating blanket. To my relief, I had found a rock to sit on, so that I was slightly elevated above the rest of the people and able to catch the odd breath of fresh air that wafted overhead.

A local speaker had given a simple outline of the Gospel. Now it was my turn to teach "doctrine." This was somewhat of a joke. I knew very little of the language. Fortunately, a senior colleague had drafted a few elementary lessons.

I stood up. "We will do the creation story," I announced. "Everybody repeat: the Creator above is good."

Hundreds of pairs of lips dutifully recited, *"At wakkagak mbogut paga obeelom wonage-o."*

"He created us."

"Nit wakkagagerak."

In fifteen brief sentences, we covered a basic Bible doctrine. After having gone through the lesson several times like this, I asked, "Who can repeat the whole story?"

A young fellow named Nggurimban got up. His face expressed a mixture of pride and self-consciousness. *"At wakkagak mbogut paga obeelom wonage-o,"* he began, *"An yikit-o."* I will say it.

He raised his right hand, fingers outstretched, and with his left hand he bent down the little finger, indicating that he had successfully completed the first sentence. Upon completion of the second sentence, the ring finger was bent down. When all ten fingers were down and some sentences still remained to be spoken, Nggurimban borrowed the hand of one of the listeners. Without hesitation he recited the whole story.

Not everybody was so quick to take it in. We concluded the service by repeating the lesson a few times.

Slowly the crowd dispersed. In the evening small groups of people would huddle around the fire in their huts and after a long period of monotonous chanting, someone would suggest reviewing the story. Everybody who was able would contribute.

"I remember Jesus died in our place," a woman might volunteer, a pleased look on her face. "Well said, my sister," an older-man would reply gently. "Well said. But that bit comes later."

So they would all sit, pondering, reconstructing—diligently and patiently working on a puzzle that was to become a Bible story. It was usually late at night by the time the complete story had been put together in the correct order. Finally, someone would repeat the whole thing one more time, bending down a finger after each completed sentence. During our next service a few more people would be able to recite the Genesis narrative.

The services were completely different from those in Europe or America

Sometimes it all seemed so futile. Our knowledge of the language was still totally inadequate and the people's comprehension minimal. What helped to make up for this, though, was their eagerness to learn. And they were learning the right things. "The word of God is quick and powerful and sharper than any two-edged sword," the Bible tells us (Hebrews 4:12). This word was doing its work in the hearts of the people.

"We never knew that God created us," Tupuwarijak volunteered as we sat together on the ground. Contrary to some bizarre beliefs among other tribes, the Danis had simply believed that their people had always existed. If there ever had been a beginning, it was too far back for them to worry about.

They were very pleased to find out about the possibility of having a relationship with an Almighty God. "And God loves us, doesn't He?" The man speaking just beamed, his face showing that he understood something of the miracle of God's love.

"Yes, He sent Jesus, who died in our place." That was Nigitandok's contribution. A boy of about fourteen (the Danis did not keep track of their age), he was very slow of understanding. But this truth had taken hold of him. Nigitandok remained a thoroughly loyal Christian and later on, against all hopes, became a dedicated, courageous, and effective missionary in the Eastern Highlands. Even in the face of a serious death-threat he was to hold his ground in the faith.

"Does God really love all of us?" someone else asked hesitantly. A neighbour answered re-affirmingly.

"But He doesn't love our enemies, does He? They're bad people!" It took some convincing that the enemies were not the only bad people, and that God loved them, too. But after some time, this truth began to sink in.

The results were extraordinary: a new spiritual reality of unknown magnitude filled the hearts of the people.

"If God created them and loves them, then we are bad people," someone announced. "God loved our enemies, but we hated them. God created them, but we killed them."

This realization was overwhelming to many of the Danis. It also caused confusion. Tribal warfare had been one of the main occupations and excitements within the Dani culture, comparable to sports in some Western cultures. They even kept a score of the number of people killed on each side. Lagging behind with 1:0 was reason enough to start another battle. A 1:1 score was of course unacceptable to both parties. As a result, battles were frequent and fierce. The number of victims never stayed the same for long. "We have always been a fighting people," someone explained.

Without warning, Lemengga stood up. This meant he felt he had something important to say. Lemengga had been working around my house as a handyman for some time. He was willing and hard-working, though not very intelligent. His face expressed the dullness of his mind.

"I have killed many people," he volunteered. He raised a gnarled hand bending down a finger for every enemy he had slain. When seven fingers were down, Lemengga fell silent. He looked at those gathered at his feet, bewildered. Having killed seven people was nothing out of the ordinary, yet Lemengga was revered for the cold-blooded fearlessness with which he always went into battle. His killings were the only thing he could be proud of.

Now, all of a sudden, people started saying that killing was bad. It was all so confusing.

But Lemengga eventually managed to figure things out for himself. On a later occasion, he once more stood up in public—contrary to his shy nature. One by one he bent down seven fingers.

"I have killed all these people," he said sadly. "I killed people whom God created and loved." Lemengga's voice quivered. A tear rolled down his ruddy cheek into his beard, quietly glistening in the light of the rising sun.

Although these developments took place over a period of time, the Dani people were very quick and radical in coming to grips with the consequences of the new spiritual reality. Their simplicity and boldness often put the faith of the missionaries to the test. Their reasoning went like this:

"If God loves our enemies like He loves us, we don't want to kill them anymore. If we're not going to kill anymore, we no longer need our bows and arrows. Seeing we don't need them, let's burn them."

I only witnessed one of the later burnings, but it is still a vivid memory.

The extreme monotony of tribal life had been broken by the introduction of names for days and months. The burning was to take place on a Sunday. From all directions small groups of people could be seen moving down narrow mountain trails towards the mission station. Every man carried his own fighting gear: bows, arrows, ten-foot long spears, war-jackets of woven bamboo, ornate shields, and bone daggers. Young boys were keen to assist in carrying the armament.

At last the weapons were all brought together on a huge pile the size of a very large tent. The people sat around it in a circle.

A hush fell over them as they recognized what a momentous occasion this was in the history of their tribe. Never before had they been able to trust anyone, for fear of being murdered. Now they were demonstrating their trust in Jesus, by surrendering their weapons to Him. Seeing He possessed the secret of Nabelan Kabelan, there was nothing to fear.

A local chief stood up and briefly addressed the silent multitude. A ripple ran through the crowd as a man emerged from a nearby hut with a burning stick in his hand. He placed it against the massive pyre. Within minutes the bone-dry materials began to snap and crackle, while a gentle breeze willingly pushed and pulled the flames into action. As thick clouds of smoke began to billow out of the roaring flames, the people began to sing. At first hesitantly, as though intimidated by the howling fire, but then, breaking the spell, their song rose to full strength—a song to the glory of the One who had brought about this impressive turning-point in their tribal existence.

"Wa Yetut, ninabuwa-nen..." "Thank you, Jesus, for loving us. Thank you, Jesus, for dying for us. Thank you, Jesus, for rising again. Thank you, Jesus, for coming back..."

After every sentence chanted by the precantor, the entire congregation would respond with a swelling, powerful, *"Wa, Yetut."*

As the last embers died away, a new thought was taking shape in the hearts of *"Ala apuri,"* God's sons in this long-forgotten valley. The thought was magnificent and terrifying at once. It was of such simple logic that it could only have come from above. And it was to set the tone for the development of the Dani church for years to come.

OLD PASSIONS

THE FACT that the Dani took their faith seriously was evident in many areas. The weapons had disappeared, and people's behavior had changed. But you couldn't demand too much at once. Much still had to be made clear through instruction and examples. Sometimes the old temperaments flared up.

Not long after a weapon-burning in Kanggyme, there was trouble in the air. A pet pig had gotten into another man's garden and caused great havoc. The man had killed the pig in revenge. This had caused quite a commotion, as he was not supposed to have a bow or arrows, although different bows were used for hunting pigs than for warfare.

The not very Christian behavior of killing the pig resulted in a not very Christian desire for revenge.

John Dekker and I rushed over to get an idea of the situation, which was already extremely tense. Small groups of men had gathered everywhere. The usual cheerful atmosphere was missing. The next steps were discussed in hushed voices.

Suddenly, a man shouted a threat or insult. The others in the group jeered in agreement. This was the end of all restraint; the voices became louder and angrier. The insults were thrown back in the same way. As there were no bows and arrows, the men began to pick up stones to settle the dispute.

The situation became more and more threatening. As in earlier days, the men challenged each other, by running back and forth. That was always the prelude to a fight.

We didn't have to think long to know what we had to do. John took one side; I took the other. "Put down the stones!" I ordered sternly, but no one moved. I stepped right up to a young man, looked him in the face and said again: "Put down the stones!"

Then the stones plopped down at my feet, and I went on to the next person: "Put the stones down!" As the man hesitated, I repeated my request. Hesitantly, he let go of one stone after the other.

At that moment, a man called Joly moved away from my group and ran towards the other men John was about to disarm. (Joly was a friendly man and had taken on the job of looking after our family when we had first arrived. When too many people crowded around us, he had managed to disperse them, at least temporarily. As a reward for this service, he had let us know that he wanted to move into our house.)

But now, his own concern seemed more important to him. I ran after him and tried to catch up with him by wrapping my arm around his neck—partly to stop him, partly to get his attention. "Joly, wait! That's not what Jesus wants you to do!" I couldn't think of anything else now. Joly did not stop. "Joly, that's not what Jesus wants you to do! Put the stones down now!"

He had finally understood me. Joly slowed down and dropped the stones. It wasn't a minute too soon. One of Joly's men had also started running and didn't look like he wanted to stop. Even when I got hold of him with my arm, he kept running. He raced towards the men in the other group with undiminished speed. On the spur of the moment, I grabbed the long yellow gourd that the men wore around their waists—and the brittle shell broke in my hand. A voice from heaven could not have been more powerful. When the man realized what had happened, he immediately tried to cover his nakedness with both hands, dropping his ammunition in the process.

Only now did the heated heads calm down and the fight ran out of steam. Several more attempts at mediation were necessary before an agreement was reached. Disaster had been averted once again.

PERILOUS PROCLAMATION

"**M**EN . . . We would like to talk to you."
A group of local chieftains had gathered at the Clarke's residence in Mamit. As usual, they were accompanied by countless inquisitive followers. Frank welcomed the delegation into his backyard and everyone squatted down on the ground.

The spokesman did not waste a single word. "We want to go to our enemies," he announced.

Frank was appalled. He had treated enough war-injuries and seen enough suffering as a result of arrow tips deeply lodged in a human body, causing ugly infections. He kept his cool nonetheless.

"Why, my friends?" he asked gently. It saddened him to think how such a step would damage the fresh spiritual life in the valley. "Why should you go back to your enemies? They are no longer enemies. God created and loves them just as He created and loves you."

All the chiefs seemed to react at once, drowning out Frank's plea.

"*A lek-o nore!* Not at all, my friend," the spokesman interrupted, his dark face radiant with joy.

"Men . . . We do want to go to our enemies. But not to kill them. We want to tell them that God created them and loves them. They too must know that Jesus wants to offer them the gift of Nabelan Kabelan."

Frank knew well enough how intricate and complicated the Dani language was: he must have misunderstood.

"My ears did not hear, my friend," he responded.

Patiently the message was repeated. Frank was not easily perturbed, but the news now conveyed to him almost took his breath away.

"To your enemies?" he asked incredulously. "First you burned your weapons and now you want to go to your enemies? They'll kill the lot of you as soon as you are within range!" Unwittingly he had raised his voice. He felt his cheeks burning. The chieftains were slightly bewildered now, too.

"But—but—our enemies are bad people," one of them said. "Because they are bad, they will go to the Great Fire. But Jesus loves them. And—therefore, we love them too."

"Nggenanibaga," another continued, addressing Frank by the Dani name given him. "You told us that if we die we will go to God's yard." (There were no words in their language for heaven or hell.) "Perhaps our enemies will kill us. Perhaps we will all die. So what? We will be going right to God's yard."

Everyone smiled approval, thinking about the wonderful prospect that might soon become reality. Frank realized there was no point in arguing. They were not going to be held back. The discussion was closed.

One of the men got up. *"Nawi o,"* he said. "Let's go." His words seemed to suggest something far more significant than simply leaving Nggenanibaga's yard.

Not long after that they set off—possibly the most unusual evangelistic band ever to set out on a mission. I was elsewhere at the time of that initial journey, but afterwards frequently traversed the same trail.

I heard the story so often that it is not difficult to visualize all that took place.

Quietly chanting, an orderly group walked away from the settlement. Outwardly they did not look much different than they would have years before. The men wore string bags on their heads to keep their hair in place. Many of them wore a pig tusk through their pierced nasal septum. Soot and pig-grease formed part of the general make-up. The men wore nothing but a long, narrow, yellow gourd to cover their private parts. Children were completely naked. Women wore string skirts made from the bark of trees. The trail led down steeply to the Toli River. The sharp descent and the excitement of the occasion soon caused the singing to stop. The only sound heard was the muffled cadence of dozens of pairs of bare feet lightly padding down the steep path.

About halfway down, the procession came to a halt at a small, but strategically important knoll. It was situated at approximately the same level as the enemy village on the opposite side of the river. In wartime this mound was the place from which to challenge and hurl insults at the enemy. After gaining attention with a long, drawn-out shout, a voice would boom across the quiet valley:

"Today we are going to get you. We are coming to kill you. We will burn down your houses. We will steal your women. We will kill your pigs."

In response, all those present would show their approval by wildly jumping up and down, hooting and hollering. After that, the whole company would go swarming down the hill, cross the river and rush up the other side towards a confrontation with the enemy.

As the self-appointed evangelists and their following reached the little hill, they realized that, as per usual, they should announce their coming.

"*Kum yikit a?*" Aganggen suggested. He was a stocky little fellow with a round face, brown eyes and powerful voice. "Shall I tell them that we are coming?"

The group nodded consent. The long, loud shout was familiar. The message that followed was not. At the top of his voice, Aganggen yelled:

"Today we are not coming to kill you. We have good news to tell you. We have found the secret of Nabelan Kabelan. We are coming to tell you. We will not kill you."

A thunderous explosion of yelling and hooting indicated the end of the message and the approval of Aganggen's companions.

"*Nawi o.* Let's go," someone shouted, and the excited throng broke into a wild stampede, down the hillside, across the river, up the bank. Onward to the enemy.

At this point, no one could have said for sure whether they would ever reach the village alive or whether they were rushing headlong into "God's yard."

The Panaga people meanwhile were terrified. Armed to the teeth, they stood close together. Some of them were trembling with fear. Almost all the women and children had sought refuge in the forest behind the village. Was this a trick? Where were the weapons? Why weren't the attackers shouting insults?

Carefully, one of the "witness men," as they were later to be called, stepped forward from among the company of unusual visitors. Gently and simply he explained his mission. Right there and then, the miracle took place. The longing to know the secret of Nabelan Kabelan was as strong for the Panaga people as it had been for the men from Mamit. The Panaga people listened intently. They accepted the message. There was no bloodshed, no fighting. What had been inconceivable for centuries was achieved that day in the name of Jesus.

"Now we are one in Jesus," the former enemies exclaimed as they hugged the messengers solemnly.

Not long after this, the Panaga people burned their weapons. "Now we must go and tell our enemies on the other side of the mountain," they decided.

Because of the missionary zeal of these primitive people, the Gospel spread rapidly throughout the entire Swart Valley. Towards the end of our first four-year term, about 90% of a population of 25,000 had become born-again Christians.

CHOCOLATE AND MBAWY

OCCASIONALLY, THE aggression and violence of a bygone era would pop up among the Christian Danis and old tempers would flare. But such incidents were rare and when they did occur usually a peaceful solution was soon found. We were not unduly concerned by these things. There was ample evidence that the Holy Spirit was at work. The people who had said about Jesus, "Who is He? We want Him," still meant business. And God was taking them at their word.

Stealing had always been one of the Dani "virtues." In the early days nothing was safe. The Danis were used to stealing. It was a habit they couldn't shake overnight.

One of the Mamit men had been a helper from the time I arrived there. He was not particularly big, but very muscular. The customary net bag covering his hair hung low over his forehead, a pair of shining brown eyes peering out from under it. A perpetual smile, exposing big, yellowish teeth, gave his face a happy and trustworthy expression. He had an outlandish name that I always forgot. Because of the light brown colour of his skin, I simply called him Chocolate. Chocolate was reliable and faithful.

Chocolate had been there when we started building our house. He dug the holes for the foundation poles. When they became too deep for him to work effectively with a spade, he brought his little boy along. Taking him by the ankles, Chocolate would suspend the boy upside down above the hole, lower him into it, wait till the boy had scooped up some sand with his hands, and then pull him up again. It was an ingenious way of working.

An ingenious way of working

Later on when the house was completed, I asked Chocolate to go to the woods and fetch material for building a fence around the chicken yard. Day after day, he would appear around noon with a load of wood. I took no notice when one day he didn't turn up. Not until he had stayed away for several days did I begin to wonder.

"What happened to Chocolate?" I asked the people ever-present in the yard. "Is he sick?"

"Perhaps he is sick, perhaps not," someone answered with customary tribal ambiguity.

"Has anybody seen him?" I persisted.

"I have seen him, but not lately," came a more useful contribution.

"He has gone funny. First he just sat in his hut without talking or eating. Now he doesn't even want to stay in his hut anymore. He just walks around through the jungle."

No one could offer an explanation for this strange behaviour. "Would someone go and bring him here? I would like to talk to him." A chorus of male voices picked up my request and urged a little boy along on the errand.

Chocolate arrived soon after that. His eyes betrayed fear. He had lost weight.

We found a quiet place to talk.

"I am a thief and I'll be thrown into the Great Fire," he said somberly and without introduction. We still had no other word for hell.

"No one needs to go to the Great Fire," I reminded him.

"I'll be going there, because I am a thief." He shuddered, then continued. "You told me to get wood. You paid me for it. It was your wood. But I took some of it for myself. When I was in the forest the next day, I heard the voice of God's true Spirit in my heart. 'You are a thief. You will go to the Great Fire.' So I did not go to the forest anymore. I stayed at home."

Chocolate looked pathetic and forlorn.

"Then what?" I prodded gently.

"The true Spirit was in my hut, too," he said. "He told me the same thing. 'You are a thief. You'll go to the Great Fire.' So I left home."

His voice was a mere whisper now, as he sat staring at the ground.

"The true Spirit is in the jungle, too," he concluded, fully convinced of the seriousness of his situation and the deserved condemnation awaiting him.

"But you have told me now," I counselled. "You can bring back the wood and ask God to forgive you. Jesus knows we are all bad people. That's exactly why He came. He loves you."

With a hesitant, shy smile, Chocolate dared to raise his eyes a little.

We prayed together, and when he left there was a new bounce in his step. Forgiven!

Mbawy was further proof that the true Spirit was at work in the Swart Valley. Mbawy was a woman. She was short and squat, with a broad face and thick lips. Her husband bore the lofty name of Ji endagembanonuwa. The outstanding thing about Mbawy was that, as a woman in the entirely male-oriented Dani society, she had decided of her own accord to respond to the love of Jesus Christ.

In the early days it had required quite a bit of reasoning to convince the men that God had created women, too. It startled the men to hear that He even loved the women, and that they were "heirs together of the grace of life" (1 Peter 3:7). Until then, women had held no status at all. They were a necessary evil, to be kept at a distance because of their alleged capacity for witch-craft. Fortunately, the forefathers had handed down a foolproof way of determining whether a woman under suspicion of such crimes against the community was really guilty or not. The suspect, usually trembling with fear, would be dragged before a council of men. Without much ado, they would quickly pronounce sentence: the woman would either be set free or riddled with arrows. The legal procedure was simple. With a sharp strip of bamboo, a smah piece of the suspect's ear would be sliced off. If the ear did not bleed, she was innocent. The slightest trace of blood meant guilt and swift death.

A cut ear almost always bled.

Once I tried to save the life of such a woman. I didn't argue against witch-craft, but against the foolishness of the procedure. The jury decided to grant the woman a hitherto unknown mercy: instead of being shot to death she was beaten so severely that she was unable to walk for days. Christianity was gaining ground!

Change came slowly. For a long time still, women were ill-treated continually. It was not uncommon for greedy relatives to sell a girl at birth to an older man. Down-payment of a couple of pigs would suffice to validate the transaction. As soon as the girl began to show signs of physical maturity, the owner would claim his purchase and a final settlement was made. Women and children lived in separate huts, away from the men but together with the domestic pigs—another part of a man's possessions.

Most women took a long time climbing up out of this deeply degraded position. Many of them had become so dull due to ill-treatment, that it seemed to matter little to them what happened with their lives. In some ways it was easier to shrug your shoulders and say, "We're only women anyway," than to assert a new position offered in Christ.

Mbawy was different. The Lord opened her heart and she responded to the Gospel with surprising keenness. She was the first woman I ever saw standing up in a meeting to testify of her faith in Christ and her assurance of salvation. She didn't find it easy. It had always been safer for women to keep a low profile. When she stood that first time, the blood was drained from her face and her lips were quivering. Her knees shook so badly that the men sitting behind her had to hold them to stop her from falling over. Even so, she spoke, testifying to what Jesus had done in her life.

Not long after that, she came to see Frank Clarke, bringing some cowrie shells with her. We had often offered the people money and trade items, but they insisted on being paid for their work in cowrie shells.

"These are not mine, but yours," Mbawy told Frank. "When you first came and we helped you to build the airstrip, we were still heathen. I used to report for work in the morning and then go off to my garden. In the afternoon I came back, rubbed some clay on my shoulders and legs to make you believe I had been working, and then collected my pay. Now I know that is stealing. That's why I am bringing these shells back to you."

Mbawy and her husband continued to grow in grace and in the knowledge of the Lord Jesus Christ. They were among the first fifty-eight believers in Mamit to be baptized. After completion of their training, they served for many years as missionaries to a tribe in the Eastern Highlands of New Guinea.

We had been among the Danis for almost one year now. The first hurdles had been taken. We had survived physically and spiritually. In both respects, we know, our survival could only be ascribed to miracles. When the day of our first anniversary on the mission field came around, I was jubilant. We had completed a full cycle!

"If you can handle one year of this, you can handle two," I encouraged myself. Indeed, though life on the field was never without hardships, in many ways we seemed to have gotten over the worst of them. And we had come out on top.

NEW NAMES, NEW HAIRSTYLES

IN THE meantime, the Holy Spirit continued His work. He did not restrict Himself to individual men and women. Recurrently, we saw evidence of His work among the entire tribe.

One example of this was the burning of weapons. The burnings had been an initiative of the people themselves. Some might argue that the Danis only did this to please the missionaries, but I am sure the opposite was the case. The people were giving heed to an inner conviction that no missionary could have planted within them. Developments proved this again and again. The people made changes in areas of life where the missionaries had not yet even penetrated. Some of these changes were impressive to say the least.

Another of these was the public confession of *"anggen kunik,"* or secret names. Unknown to us, young boys were customarily given secret names as a part of their initiation into manhood. Sometimes these were names of ancestors, other times they seemed to have no direct meaning. The *anggen kunik* were believed to have magic powers. A man would sooner go to battle unarmed than without the protection of his secret name. In the midst of the fight he could gain help and victory by whispering his secret name. This was not easy, however, as the name would lose its power if it ever became known to anyone else. Utter secrecy was essential. We were unaware of this bulwark of Satan until the Danis themselves exposed it to us. They went about tearing it down in their usual bold and simplistic way.

"We are never going to fight anymore, so what is the use of these names?" they reasoned. "Besides, we now have the name of Jesus, which is better than any other name."

After Sunday services, frequently a few men would get up and bear witness to that effect. Then they would publicly confess their *anggen kunik*. Some whispered them in a barely audible voice. Others shouted them out triumphantly, confidently stating their reasons for doing so. The congregation sat motionless and listened as the powers of darkness were forced to retreat.

Immediately following the confession of the *anggen kunik,* another joyful event took place, as the Danis felt more and more secure under the protection of their faithful friend Jesus. This next change, unlike previous ones, did not spread across the tribe gradually. It was a one-time affair in which all the men participated.

One quiet afternoon a delegation of four men came to see me.

They were chiefs of nearby villages. I knew them well. One of them had a fragment of a china saucer hanging around his neck. He had found it somewhere and with great patience bored a hole in it and attached it to a piece of string, thus transforming a piece of white man's waste into a much admired and coveted ornament. The man had strikingly gentle eyes. His speech and movements were slow. Because of these characteristics, I had nicknamed him Flying Saucer.

Flying Saucer cleared his throat. "Kanggipaga" (he used the name the people had given me) "we would like you to cut the hair of the four of us. And tomorrow all our friends—very many of them—will be coming to have their hair cut, too."

A happy smile spread across his friendly face. He was obviously doing me a great honour in asking this. Why, I was not sure. I needed an explanation. Grinning contentedly, Flying Saucer complied.

"Men . . . We do not need our hair anymore."

This didn't make things much clearer. But it was a start.

"You see, Kanggipaga," the old chief continued, "Kanggipaga, our hair, well, what shall I say?" He wasn't the least bit bothered by his inability to express himself.

"Well, Kanggipaga, we think you ought to cut our hair." His speech suddenly gained momentum. "Our hair, Kanggipaga—we used it to worship evil spirits. This is how we did it."

Flying Saucer let his head rest on his right shoulder, then swung it over to his left shoulder and back again in quickening motion. His thick long hair would have started flying wildly had it not been kept in place by a net bag. "We used to take off our nets," he went on. "It pleased the spirits."

"Yes, that is what we used to do," the three companions agreed.

"But now we know Jesus," Flying Saucer beamed blissfully. "We are through with the evil spirits. We want to follow Jesus. That is why we don't need our hair anymore. You told us about Jesus, so all the men are coming to you tomorrow. Only the four of us want ours cut today."

I looked into four pairs of expectant eyes. How could I resist? "My friends, what you have asked me to do will be my delight." Immediately I was embraced by eight dark arms.

"My friend, you are good, Kanggipaga."

While I went inside to get the scissors, the men took the nets off their hair. I had never seen them like that before. Their long, matted hair was absolutely filthy, covered with grease, grime, and grit. When the job was done, my scissors were blunt. I could hardly recognize the men as they admired each other's avant-garde coiffure.

Before returning to their villages, they reminded me, "You are the one who told us about Jesus. Tomorrow all of our men will come for a haircut."

Early the next morning the yard was filled with men. Hundreds of them. Most of them had already removed their net bags in anticipation of the solemn event. The hair of some men reached down to their knees. Suddenly, I could understand the stories I had heard about rats trying to make nests in the men's hair while they slept.

One old gentleman, Mburumburu was rather embarrassed. He had taken off his net, only to discover that he had hardly any hair left.

When I stepped outside a hush fell over the crowd. "My friends, thank you for coming here," I began. "I am glad you want to follow Jesus in every way. There are many more words I want to speak to you about Jesus. But first I must learn how to say them in your language. Then I will be able to tell you more. If I must cut your hair for many days, I will not be able to teach. I have cut the hair of some of you. Why don't you now cut each other's hair?"

To my relief, the men agreed with this suggestion, after some bustle amongst themselves. Before long, little groups of men had formed all over the compound, sitting on their haunches hacking away at each other's hair with sharp strips of bamboo.

Recently cut hair, ready to be burned

When all had had their turn, the hair was gathered together in a huge pile to be burned. The initial hilarity soon dissipated and a spirit of gratitude and adoration settled upon the men as they sat around the mass of hair. One of them had the honourable task of setting it alight. As the fire blazed, the men thoughtfully chanted a favorite tune:

"Thank you, Jesus, for loving us. Thank you, Jesus, for untying our bonds . . ."

The roaring flames coughed thick billows of green, grey, and black smoke that gently wafted heavenward. The almost unbearable stench of scorched, burning hair must have arrived in heaven as a sweet-smelling savour to Christ (Philippians 4:18). *"Wa Jetut."* Thank you, Jesus.

We want to follow Jesus . . . that's why we don't need our hair anymore

THE BIG PLUNGE

It was almost impossible to believe that the spontaneous and wholehearted Dani response to our message was not the work of the Holy Spirit. We had simply repeated what Peter preached at Pentecost: "Repent." And the Danis, obviously completely ignorant of the New Testament history, had reacted almost exactly according to the Scriptural pattern of Acts 2:37-47, "Men and brethren, what shall we do?"

Despite this evidence, questions as to the authenticity of the spiritual awakening in the Swart Valley remained. What if the whole thing wasn't genuine? Did the people really understand the Gospel?

Once I was called out of my bed at five o'clock in the morning. A man was sitting at my doorstep, puzzled and concerned. He was from an outlying area. I never had seen him before. He scarcely took time for exchanging the customary greetings.

"Kanggipaga," he began. "I really believe. I know that Jesus gave me Nabelan Kabelan. But yesterday my piglet died. Did it not have eternal life?"

I was baffled at the question. To be honest, it was an exception. But how could we be sure that all those Danis who did not voice such questions truly understood the gift of God?

At one time, the rumour began to circulate that eventually the skin of every active believer would turn white. Here, too, the inference was evident. Being white meant being wealthy. White people wore clothes. They appear to have access to unimaginable riches: whenever they needed something they just spoke into the radio and within a few weeks the desired items would drop from the sky in a steel bird. When the plane departed again, no cash had changed hands, not even a pig was loaded onto the plane to settle the account.

What exactly did the Danis have in mind when they accepted the Gospel? Did they regard it as some kind of business deal? Were they expecting to receive material goods in return for having burned their weapons, confessed their *anggen kunik,* and cut off their hair?

We often questioned them on these things. They always insisted that their sole desire was Nabelan Kabelan.

Now we faced something of a dilemma. Peter had not only preached repentance. He had also urged his listeners to be baptized. We had certainly taught the doctrine of baptism. But the question was how to go about applying this doctrine. There was no comparison between the people Peter had addressed and those we were dealing with.

Hesitantly, as though it were a test case, we decided to baptize a few people we knew intimately. On February 23, 1964, the first baptism in Mamit took place. Fifty-eight believers had passed the simple test we had compiled for them.

Interest in the baptismal service was overwhelming. Some five thousand people showed up. Just before the service, there was an amusing incident that helped to relax the atmosphere a little. Together with the candidates, I was sitting by the pool that had been dug for the occasion, when a stately rooster strutted onto the scene. With an air of grave self-importance, it paraded amongst the congregation seated on the ground. Chickens had been unknown in the Swart Valley until we imported them. They were treated with the necessary respect. Suddenly the bird jumped up and landed on the head of one of the candidates. Already somewhat nervous, the poor man didn't know what to do, how to react. Fortunately, one of the older men offered some sage advice.

"Leave it! Leave it!" he exclaimed. "For when Jesus was baptized, there was also a bird which came to sit on His head."

I don't know how long that bird remained on the Sacred Head, but I must admit I was quite relieved when the rooster decided to hop off to find a different roosting place.

The baptisms did not affect the people in a negative way at all. They continued to display devoted loyalty and sincerity of faith. Four months later another sixty-three believers were baptized.

The first three elders (from left): Tuwanonuwa, Andugumanggen, and Kabutna

Next, we decided that the local church should have its own indigenous leadership. Frank and I agreed that at least three men should share this responsibility. We were eager to involve the baptized believers in the election of their own elders. It did pose a bit of a problem. We felt each person should be able to vote secretly, but at that time hardly anyone could write and secret ballots were out of the question. We resolved the issue as follows: having explained that the three best men should become leaders, we told everyone to take time to pray about the matter. Then, on a set day, they would come individually to tell me who they thought was the most suitable person for the office.

The day came. I sat down some fifty feet away from where the voters had gathered, and invited each member to come forward and let me know whom he or she wished to see elected. They certainly had flair for ceremony. Slowly, one by one, they arose and in a dignified manner walked over to where I was seated. At first I thought they were playing a joke. But their faces indicated how serious they were as quite a number of them solemnly whispered in my ear, "I am the best one in the congregation."

Ah well, we took the whole exercise as a general rehearsal and organized another election. This time it worked. Tuwanonuwa, Andugumanggen, and Kabutna were chosen.

They were an amazing trio. Each of them had left behind him a background marked by cruelty, hatred, and murder. Together they had killed roughly twenty-five people before becoming Christians. But God's grace did its remarkable work. The three men executed their job admirably. Until this day, all three are loyal and beloved leaders.

It wasn't until July 1965 that we finally dared to take the big plunge. Frank and Betty Clarke had been on furlough for almost one year and we were planning to go on our first furlough as soon as they returned. During that time I was challenged by a group of believers I had been teaching during the past years.

"Why don't you baptize us?" they demanded.

I was at a loss for words.

"Is there anything in our lives to hinder you from doing it?" There really was not. For almost four years now, they had faithfully and loyally followed their Lord as well as they knew how.

"You taught us about baptism," they said, as though I needed reminding. "So why don't you baptize us?"

It was a good question. And clever, too: they had placed the responsibility squarely on my shoulders. I had no adequate reply to the question. All of our fears had proven ungrounded. The people followed the Lord wholeheartedly. They were not looking for favours in return for their Christian service. Their keen insight and understanding of the Scriptures often amazed me.

"Why don't you baptize us?"

I was glad we finally had to face up to the question. Right there and then, I confessed: apart from perhaps my own unbelief, there was no valid reason for putting off their baptism.

A hectic time commenced when I announced that each of the eight thousand inhabitants of the Mamit area would be given the opportunity to request baptism.

At each of the various existing preaching points we asked local brethren to conduct preliminary questioning. Each prospective candidate was to be checked on three points: assurance of salvation, personal testimony in the community, elementary knowledge of Scripture.

Those who passed this test would be re-examined by a group of baptize believers from Mamit—myself, Tuwanonuwa, Andugumanggen, and Kabutna formed part of this team.

It was exciting to be travelling from one preaching point to another, accompanied by the usual followers. We would chatter and laugh and sing, the sound of our voices accompanied by the light patter of feet on the trail. In the early morning hours, the tropical sun still showed kindness. Fresh dew covered slopes and valleys with a soft, greyish-white blanket, stitched with myriads of glittering pearls and diamonds. The day ahead promised to be a good one.

"I have never been here before," someone would share. "This used to be enemy territory. But that is past now. We are one in Jesus." This last statement was often joyfully uttered by many lips at once. The new unity in Jesus was such a daily reality in the war-torn Dani culture—it just had to be proclaimed, again and again.

Heading north from the station, I usually walked for about an hour and a half. Then, after a stiff climb, we would stop for a brief rest and a bite to eat.

"This is the hill of Kanggipaga," the people joked.

"Then we'd better name it after him," someone proposed. And from then on the place was known as *"Kanggiput,"* the hilltop of Kanggipaga.

The company started to move again. Now it went downhill, skipping over mud, dirt, and rocks until we reached the river in the valley. After a quick dip in the fresh mountain stream, we began the ascent up the other side.

Without any more peaks to obstruct our view, we could see in the distance a sure sign that we were expected. "They have started the fire already." Almost imperceptibly, the pace quickened and spirits rose as we anticipated arriving at the next village.

Our visit was a special occasion and therefore had to be celebrated. A few days before our arrival, the men of the village would gather firewood and rocks. They placed the wood in a neat pile, some seventy feet long and ten feet wide. Twigs, dry leaves and grass were stuffed underneath. Stones formed the top.

On the day of the feast, large pits were dug, about ten feet in diameter and a couple of feet deep. The men did the digging while the women went to the woods and their gardens to collect ferns, leaves, and edibles. The leaves served a dual purpose: they were to line the pits so that the food would remain clean, and they formed a protective layer between the food and the stones, keeping the food from burning.

On top of the leaves, a variety of delicacies would be placed

The crackling fire was a sure sign that preparations were well under way. Soon the women would be back to line the pits. On top of the leaves, a variety of delicacies would be placed: oddly shaped sweet potatoes, shiny yellowish-green cucumbers, unripe bananas, and, of course, the succulent green leaves of the sweet potato plant. On top of all the vegetables and fruit came the pork, chicken, occasionally some fish, carefully wrapped in banana leaves and tied with vines to prevent it from disintegrating. Finally the pit was closed with additional leaves and hot rocks. By this time, our company of visitors had usually arrived and while the food was steam-cooking and enticing scents wafted across the meeting place, the people would sit down for a service.

Once, as a novice still unaccustomed to the difficult mountain trails, I had arrived at a feast quite late and exhausted. The food had been cooking for a long time and rain was threatening. The people sat around, waiting for my Bible talk. But I was just too tired. After greeting them, I told them to just go ahead with the feast, because I first wanted to rest a little.

"Did you come all this way to sleep?" one of them asked in honest disbelief. "We are waiting to hear about Jesus," another added somewhat impatiently. There was no point in arguing. I gave a short and simple message. The people were enthralled.

When after twenty minutes I sat down, several people responded. "Tell us some more," they shouted. "I don't know anymore," I replied. "I am just too tired." They would not let me off the hook. "Then tell us the same story again," someone suggested. "It was so beautiful."

How could I refuse such an eager audience? I shared some more, uplifted and refreshed by their keen interest. At last I managed to persuade them that the food would spoil in the pits and the rain would catch us out if we did not proceed.

My musings came to an end as our group of walkers reached the village that morning. After the service the women opened the pits while men hurried back and forth handing out the steaming food.

One of the men asked a blessing over our meal in a loud voice: "Thank you, Father. You have given us all these sweet potatoes, the bananas, the cucumbers, the pork, the salt." He suddenly hesitated and fell silent. Eyes still tightly closed, he inquired under his breath, "What else have we got?"

"Beans," someone volunteered.

"And thank you for the beans, Father. In Jesus' name, Amen." "Amen," the entire congregation chorused.

Then we ate. Juices and flavours had been preserved marvellously in this ingenious way of cooking. For a while little else could be heard but gulping and smacking. Friends exchanged tidbits. I was usually given enough to feed an orphanage. When I distributed what I could not eat, I was praised for my generosity.

At last, as the sun had already long since reached its zenith, the time had come for the examination of the baptism candidates. Together with the elders who had come with me from Mamit and some of the local leaders, we withdrew to the quietness of a hut. One by one the applicants appeared. Some were very nervous, others radiated confidence. An old man came in, greeting each of us separately, and then sitting down cross-legged on the mud floor. He looked at us expectantly.

"Well, my father," I said, paying due respect to his age, "can you tell us why Jesus came into this world?"

It was a simple, standard question, so I received a simple, standard answer.

"What does it mean to you personally that Jesus came into this world?" I proceeded.

The man's face lit up. "Nggenanibaga once told us a story about Lazarus," he began, waving vaguely in the direction of Mamit, evidently the scene of the events he was about to recount.

"He said that Lazarus had died and was wrapped in grave clothes. He said that we were dead like Lazarus and that our sins were wrapped around us like those clothes. But Jesus came and made Lazarus alive again. Nggenanibaga said that Jesus could make us alive again, too."

He paused for a moment, as if to review what he had just said. When he opened his mouth again, he was no longer echoing a missionary but speaking from his own personal experience.

"After the service I went to my hut. I said, 'Jesus, I am all tied up with sin, like Lazarus. Will you please untie me?'" The memory of this event brought joy-lights to the man's gentle eyes. A broad smile swept across his aging face. He ended his testimony quietly, but triumphantly. "He did."

There was really no need for further questions. This simple testimony thrilled us all. My co-workers beamed. "Our hearts are telling us that our father knows Jesus," they said. We agreed unanimously that he should be baptized.

Next was a woman. Her nervousness could not hide the glimmerings of new life within her. After she had struggled through the examination, I asked my fellow-examiners for their opinion. They all said the same thing: "Her words are weak, but in her heart she knows Jesus."

"Shall we baptize her then?" There was a short silence. Then everyone consented. "I think so, too." I nodded to the woman. Immediately she jumped up, rushed over to where I was sitting, grabbed my arm, and began to cover it with little bites, uttering praise to God as she did so. "She is showing you that she loves you," the men explained obligingly.

The teenage girl who walked in next was flashing with self-confidence. The way she moved her hips and let her grass skirt swing indicated but one thing: she knew she was going to make it.

"We'd better get out the heavy guns," I told myself. The men caught on immediately. The girl answered some relatively difficult questions glibly and without effort. She was sure of herself. There wasn't a question she couldn't answer and she spoke with self-assurance and untarnished pride. She scored high on all parts of the exam.

"Shall we baptize her?" I asked the men, carefully trying to conceal my own conviction. All heads shook in disagreement.

"Why not?" I asked in feigned surprise. "She knows all the answers."

Andugumanggen looked troubled. "She knows all the answers," he agreed, "but she has a big liver." He was using a colloquial expression we all understood: the girl was proud.

When we told her we did not think she was ready for baptism, she was very offended, and marched off with swinging hips. I marvelled at the men's wisdom.

The white-haired, bent-over man whose turn had now come was deaf and dumb. He sat down with difficulty. Andugumanggen motioned him to speak to me. The sounds he produced were unintelligible, but his facial expressions and gestures spoke volumes. We experienced the unity of the Spirit and let him pass unanimously—even though he had not even been able to pronounce the name of Jesus.

The day was well advanced when the last candidate left our hut. A spirit of joy and gratitude rested on the people as we announced the names of those who would be baptized at the next service.

Loaded with gifts of left-over food, we started the homeward journey. We were already nearing the station when without saying anything one of the men separated himself from the group. He jumped over a fence erected to keep pigs out of the gardens and made his way to a woman working there. We saw him greet her respectfully and warmly. After a brief conversation, he handed her the big chunk of pork he had received for himself at the feast that day. Meat was rarely available and therefore much desired among the Danis—this was a huge present.

"Why did you give all that meat away?" I wondered aloud when the man had rejoined us.

"When we were still enemies, I killed her husband," he said. "But now we love each other in Jesus."

STEADFAST CONTINUANCE

We were running short of time. Requests for baptism came pouring in from all over the valley. We managed to visit every area to question candidates, but it seemed impossible to return to each place for the actual baptismal service. To solve the problem, I decided we would organize one large service at the Mamit station. And a large service it was. On the day before the baptism, there was a grand feast. Some five thousand people attended. More than two hundred pigs were slaughtered and cooked. The next morning, July 11, 1965, we conducted the fifth and largest baptismal service ever held in Mamit. Six hundred sixty-three people symbolically descended into the water-grave to rise up again in newness of life (Romans 6:3-4).

After a little more than four years, there were now eight hundred and seventy-one baptized believers in the Mamit area. Thousands of others had publicly confessed to have assurance of salvation. Ordered lives gave clear evidence of the astounding changes that had taken place in many hearts.

Still, even after the mass baptism, a little fear lingered in my heart. There was no doubt about it: to many of the Danis, being baptized was something of a status symbol. Now that many had attained to this status, would their devotion to Christ and His word begin to slacken?

My apprehension proved groundless. Once again, before our very eyes, we saw a true-to-life reproduction of the developments of the First Church. Of course the Dani Christians were totally unaware of this striking resemblance. In fact, it wasn't until years later that I myself recognized what had taken place.

People symbolically descended into the water-grave to rise up again in newness of life.

Immediately following the baptismal service in Mamit, local churches had been established on different locations throughout the area. If there were at least thirty baptized believers and three men could be found capable of shepherding this flock, a new church came into being. For each additional thirty believers, a new elder was appointed. These elders came to the mission compound in Mamit regularly to be instructed. During the weekends they spent time with their own congregations. Like the First Church, "they continued steadfastly in the apostles' doctrine" (Acts 2:42).

Church services with five thousand people in attendance were no longer common, though on special occasions the people still loved to get together in large numbers.

Service in front of the first church in Mamit

Being split up into smaller groups was at first not appreciated by everyone. One incident brought this to light. It was Sunday. I was standing in front of a group of hundreds of believers. For some time I had felt we should start organizing smaller services to meet the specific needs of various groups of people. At the conclusion of our service that Sunday, I unfolded my plan.

"I will reveal what I have thought," I began, picking up the native idiom, and then proceeding to explain the idea of subdivisions.

My proposal was met with stony silence. My "revelation" was not pleasing to the people. Was I trying to undermine their new-found unity in Christ by separating men, women, and young people? They seemed to think so. "Never mind," I thought. "They will understand when they see how it works."

I continued to outline my strategy. "Tomorrow is *Tomban eeppunuk.*" *Tomban eeppunuk* stood for Monday. It literally means, "after prayers," indicating it is the day after Sunday, "the day of prayers."

"*Tomban eeppunuk,* shortly before it is time to eat potato leaves, we will have a meeting just for the young people. They are the only ones that are to come. For the others, we will have meetings at other times. Does everybody understand?"

"*E o.*" The response was not very convincing. I repeated what I had just said. "Does everybody understand?"

"*E o.*"

I dismissed the congregation.

Tomban eeppunuk, shortly before the time for eating potato leaves, I looked out of my window. Outside it was as busy as it was every Sunday. I watched the people as they slowly filed into the newly erected, thatch-covered church building. A few minutes later I joined them. The place was packed with people of all ages.

"Did you not understand that this was going to be a service for young people only?" I enquired gently.

Mburumburu got to his feet at once. He was the one who had discovered on the day of hair-cutting and burning that he was virtually bald. Now he wore the green field hat that I had given him to protect his bald pate from the beating sun. He wore the hat almost day and night. As he peered at me now from underneath its wide, floppy brim, there was alarm in his eyes. His thin grey beard quivered as he opened his mouth, still searching for the right words. "Jesus did not die for the young people only." Mburumburu spoke firmly now, admonishingly. "He died for all of us. We all want to hear more about Him."

A rumble of approval rolled through the congregation. The old man sat down, determined to see his admonition heeded.

I had no choice. Grateful for their enthusiasm, I told them about our lovely Lord Jesus until it was well beyond the time for eating potato leaves.

SNATCHED FROM DESTRUCTION

"**K**ANGGIPAGA *wa e!*" Outside my little study in Mamit, an urgent voice attempted to draw my attention.

"Kanggipaga, come quickly," the man pleaded. "There is a large bird of prey in your chicken yard."

Hearing that, I immediately shoved my papers aside, grabbed my .22 rifle and a handful of bullets and was on my way. This was more fun than studying Dani grammar.

We cautiously approached the chicken yard. Those chickens were my pride and joy. I had privately ordered one hundred newly hatched chicks to be delivered via air mail from Australia. After raising them, I intended to give twenty different villages five fowl each. I had no intention of letting a hungry bird of prey wreck my pet project.

We reached the yard quickly. There wasn't a bird in sight.

"He is gone," the man said disappointedly, looking up at the treetops.

"Because you lied to me, I'll have to shoot you," I said jestingly, and pointed the barrel of my gun in his direction. It was the worst thing I could have done. Lying was a sensitive subject. To be accused of having lied to a missionary was a grave insult. And my silly suggestion that I was going to shoot the good man made matters even worse. He was deeply offended and declared that even when they were still heathen, the Danis had never aimed their weapons at a friend. Not even for fun. Now he was a Christian. And as for me, I was not only a Christian but also a missionary and a teacher. How could I do such a thing? He went on and on about it. I listened in silence, meanwhile unloading my magazine. He was right. I was sincerely sorry about the incident.

"Look," I interrupted, when still he showed no sign of ending his speech. "There is no need for you to be upset any longer. I was only joking. We are just different in this respect: we don't mind pointing guns at each other if it's just for fun."

Our eldest son John Mark had been following the proceedings with great interest. He had been born about ten months earlier under the most primitive circumstances. A roughly made wooden table in a hut with a grass roof fror which "bugs and bits" kept dropping down functioned as "delivery table." The hut was situated between two warring villages. Shouts, war cries and threats of a pending attack could be clearly heard. About ten minutes before the delivery took place Jean Crowe, an Australian nurse, who had walked in from some distance, arrived. A healthy baby boy was born, but within days he developed impetigo due to the filth all around us. We fully expected him to die. Then his little sister got the same dreadful skin problem. Due to an infection on my leg, I could barely walk and that only with great pain—not very favourable conditions for a mother recovering from child birth. And of course, there were no visitors, no cards, no phone calls, no flowers. Even the little native boy who supplied us with firewood and drinking water had fled because of the dangerous situation. For our little, inexperienced missionary family, these were undoubtedly the darkest days of our entire ministry in New Guinea. We felt very much alone.

The rough, unhygienic start in life had caused John Mark no harm, however. He was a chubby, healthy little fellow with a merry twinkle in his big brown eyes. A profusion of snow-white curls framed his tanned features.

"Look," I continued to the man, who was becoming slightly belligerent. "Look, I don't even mind training a rifle at my own boy." To make my point and appease the man, I was about to pull the trigger. Then it happened.

"Don't!" A voice spoke out in clear, crisp English. John Mark had not said it—he was proudly gazing at the gun barrel pointed at his round tummy. My wife Ruth was not around. In fact, there was absolutely no one else in the neighbourhood who could have uttered this clear English phrase, simple as it was.

Slightly shaken, I withdrew my weapon and slid back the bolt. A bullet snapped out of the barrel!

It was a sobering experience. If that unknown, urgent voice had not warned me, I would have shot my own child! It was also a penetrating reminder that the Author of the book of Acts was still able and willing to perform signs and wonders. I pledged that I would never again aim a gun at anyone. Not even for fun.

That incident drew me closer to the Lord. In a new and different way I had become deeply indebted to Him.

"But many other signs truly did Jesus in the presence of His disciples" (John 20:30). Another of the many signs we witnessed during our time in New Guinea was the powerful deliverance of Angginonukwe.

Shortly before she was due to be baptized, the three elders, Tuwanonuwa, Andugumanggen, and Kabutna, came to see me about her.

"Angginonukwe has gone funny," they announced matter-of-factly. "We think she has an evil spirit."

Something inside me raised alarm. Could a Christian be possessed by an evil spirit? "Tell me all about her." I was more than curious.

"Well, it all started as soon as you passed her to be baptized," Tuwanonuwa began. I seemed to sense a hint of sarcasm in his voice. "She has taken off her grass skirt and is running around the forest," Kabutna added. Andugumanggen, a shepherd at heart, was concerned about the physical wellbeing of one of his flock.

"She has not eaten or slept for days."

"Try to catch her and bring her here so I can talk to her," I decided abruptly. The men took off as if they were going on an exciting hunt.

Soon—much too soon for my liking—a procession came to a halt in my front yard. The elders were carrying Angginonukwe and unceremoniously dumped her on the ground. A large cluster of people gathered around her. The wicked expression on her unwashed face reminded me of the state many Dani women had been in prior to conversion. Her eyes rolled wildly, flashing with a strange mixture of hatred and terror. When I came near, she began to claw ferociously, her mouth spitting out vile language and foam.

Although I had no experience whatsoever in this area, I was certain that this was some kind of demon-possession. "She has an evil spirit," I declared, perhaps more to myself than to the onlookers.

A hush fell over the crowd. Suddenly I was overcome by a wave of loneliness, as the implications of what I had just said imprinted themselves upon my mind. I knew that everyone saw the connection between Angginonukwe's desire to be baptized and her present condition. The powers of darkness were presenting a terrifying challenge. And if I did not meet it and overcome it in the power of Christ, we might as well pack our bags and go home. Who would want to be baptized if it meant becoming subject to the wrath of evil spirits? If our work among the Danis was to continue at all, the Lordship of Jesus Christ needed to be established very emphatically. The significance of the occasion was crystal clear. I had to take action.

"Angginonukwe has an evil spirit," I reiterated. It was old hat to the crowd. They had been sure of it before I was. What interested them was to see how I would handle it. No one stirred. Tension mounted.

"Jesus Christ is stronger than evil spirits." I spoke loud and clear, expecting to break the tension. Nothing happened. Nobody moved. The people required more than just words. I felt the need for support. Turning to the elders, I said, "Do you believe that Jesus is stronger than evil spirits?"

What had never happened before, happened at that moment. The elders very deliberately let me down. They were not prepared to commit themselves with the stakes as high as they were.

Tuwanonuwa spoke for the others. "You told us He is."

I felt like backing out myself, but I couldn't. "Do you believe that Jesus Christ can cast out this spirit?" I repeated. All three elders answered this time, but only to verbalize the doubt I could read in their eyes. "You told us He can."

"Do you believe that Jesus can do it now?" I was growing more and more anxious.

"You told us He can."

"Let's pray," I announced tersely.

All present dutifully bowed their heads and closed their eyes. In the name of Jesus, I commanded the evil spirit to come out of Angginonukwe, to leave her alone and to depart from our area.

As soon as I opened my eyes, I saw she was different. Her facial features were relaxed. Her eyes had lost that wild glare. When I spoke, she reacted.

"Say 'Thank you, Jesus,'" I ordered.

"Wa Jetut," she responded in her native tongue.

I could have jumped for joy and expected Angginonukwe to do the same. But I was in for a surprise. As soon as she had said, *"Wa Jetut,"* she closed her eyes. For a terrifying moment I thought she had died. She had merely fallen asleep. Sound asleep. For days on end the evil spirit had tortured and exhausted her. She had been running around, screaming without a moment's rest. She hadn't eaten, hadn't slept. Now she was free. Free to sleep in peace. That was evidently what she needed most.

The elders picked her up and carried her to her hut, where she slept for more than twenty-four hours. When she woke up, she was ravenous. She ate so much that she upset her stomach and was unable to attend the baptismal service. Angginonukwe was baptized during the next service. When we left the field in 1974 she was still in fellowship.

The experience of Angginonukwe did much to bolster the faith of the Dani believers. Their confidence in the Lord Jesus grew and they became more eager to relate the Scriptures to their own lives. They would often come to me and, referring to a certain passage of the Bible, ask, "Is this for us, too?" When I answered in the affirmative, they would go off like children who had just been given a new toy. And they used their toys! Many sick were healed. Evil spirits, sometimes in visible shapes, were cast out. One Sunday I was sick myself. I sent word to the elders that I would not be able to speak because of the pain in my throat. Within minutes, the elders appeared at my home. They oozed enthusiasm.

"We will pray and then you will be able to come," they exclaimed confidently. I was hardly in the mood for sharing their excitement. But when the time came for the service, there was absolutely nothing the matter with me or my throat. I could speak normally and felt as fit as a fiddle. To stay home on grounds of sickness would have been downright dishonest. So I went to church and preached. Andugumanggen, Tuwanonuwa, and Kabutna were sitting in the front row. They were all smiles. Their eyes twinkled as if to say, "We told you so, Kanggipaga."

Sometimes I wondered who was teaching whom.

"I AM THE DEAD MAN"

KARUBAGA WAS the first station in the Swart Valley to be opened, back in 1957. Our little family had its first few days there upon arrival in the interior of New Guinea. Later on, from 1966 to 1974, we were stationed there.

Karubaga was the village in which Leenggwa was an elder. Leenggwa was an older man. In a society where the average life expectancy was about thrity-seven years, anybody over fifty was ancient.

Leenggwa was quiet and unassuming. He regularly came to our home to deliver some fresh vegetables he had grown for us in his own little garden. In all his simplicity, he was a spiritual man. The people marvelled at him. "How is it that our father Leenggwa, who can neither read nor write, knows so much about God?" they would wonder.

One day, after delivering a net bag full of fresh tomatoes at our doorstep, Leenggwa asked to talk to me. Instead of the usual "Men . . . ," Leenggwa had his own way of indicating a pause before starting to speak, or filling in a blank between two sentences. He always said, *"Yoke,"* the Dani word for yes.

"Yoke, Kanggipaga an amby mbuuluk yokkirikit o," he began. "Yes, Kanggipaga, I want to talk a little to you . . . Did you hear about Lenwarit?"

Lenwarit was a local elder. I had not heard anything in particular about him.

"Lenwarit was dead and he has become alive again." Leenggwa beamed genially. I loved that expression of serene joy that always rested on his furrowed face.

"I did not know that Lenwarit was ill," I replied, "but I am glad he is better now." When a person was seriously ill, the Danis referred to him as being "like dead."

"You don't understand," Leenggwa resumed patiently. "He was really dead, but now he is alive again." Leenggwa threw his arms up in the air, dropped his head, and let his tongue hang out of his mouth in an attempt to imitate a dead person.

I had been with the tribe for more than ten years now. In other tribes I had seen people declared dead when they were only unconscious or in a coma. For fear of death and the unknown, their fellow-tribesmen would quickly dispose of such people. The Danis however were quite different. When they said a person was dead, he was dead.

"Lenwarit rose from the dead," Leenggwa elucidated, using a different expression than before. Still puzzled, I asked him to explain.

"*Yoke*..." He smiled contentedly. "Lenwarit became alive again through the power of Jesus. He was very, very sick. Then he died. We all cried very much. Even though we would see our brother again in God's yard, we cried. We loved our brother. We still needed him. He was a good elder."

Leenggwa stopped speaking, to reflect on his own words. When he spoke up again, his voice was brimming with a new warmth and excitement.

"'If we still need our brother, why don't we ask our heavenly Father to make him alive again?' someone suggested. And someone else said, 'Jesus was dead and became alive again. And He rose up Lazarus too, and the widow's little boy!' After that, everybody agreed that we should ask Jesus to raise up Lenwarit. The hut was full of men. Lenwarit's corpse lay stretched out on the floor. For a long time we asked Jesus to make our brother alive again. We all prayed very hard. But nothing happened." Leenggwa shook his head thoughtfully, reliving the battle that had taken place.

"*Yoke*..." he repeated, "nothing happened at all. We prayed all night, but nothing happened. At dawn some of the younger men got up. 'Our heavenly Father will not answer our prayers this time', they said. 'We will get wood to cremate our brother.' I said that we should pray once more. When we did, Lenwarit began to move. He sat up! Then he looked around and said, 'I am very hungry. Are there any potatoes?' He had become alive again! He was not even sick anymore!" Leenggwa's voice was triumphant. As an afterthought, he added, "Tonight I will bring him here for you to see. The people are deeply astounded. Many have confessed sins and made things right with God." Leenggwa became silent. "Now I have finished talking and I will go home."

He slung his empty net bag over his shoulder and sauntered off. In the evening he was back, with Lenwarit.

"I am the dead man," Lenwarit introduced himself cheerfully and not without a little pride. He actually did not have much to say, as he had been totally unaware of what was going on.

"'Did you see anything while you were dead?" I wanted to know.

He had not seen anything.

"Did you hear anything?"

"Not at all, my father; it was just as when I slept."

There was not much else to say. Soon the two elders went on their way.

Around that time, reports reached me of three or four similar occurrences. I talked to one more man who, according to his own testimony as well as that of others, had been dead. I knew the man and met him regularly. He was a born-again believer. I heard too late about what was happening to go and investigate for myself.

The people had never come to tell me about it. And why should they? Before that time they had come and asked, "Can Jesus raise Dani people like He raised Lazarus?" with fear and trembling I had told them He could. And that was all they needed. They knew I never lied to them and, more importantly, that the Word of God could be trusted. So why should they come and tell me every time their prayers were answered? It was simply part of the Christian experience. And that was that!

EVERYTHING IN COMMON

IN THE Acts of the Apostles we read: "But all who believed were together and had everything in common." (Acts 2:44) In the next verse we learn how this came about: they "sold their possessions and goods and distributed them to all, according to each one's need." (Acts 2:45) I am convinced that these first believers gave so generously because their hearts were in it. They had experienced how gracious God was to them and wanted to respond in a similar way. About fifty years later, the Apostle Paul had to admonish the Christians in Corinth: ". . . each one [give] not with grudging or under compulsion, for God loves a cheerful giver." (2 Corinthians 9:7)

He who gives cheerfully focuses above all on what he can give and not on what is left for himself. His secret is that he has first given himself to the Lord. This was also the attitude of the churches in Macedonia: ". . . that in the midst of great trials the excess of their joy and their deep poverty overflowed into the riches of their generosity." (2 Corinthians 8:2)

Before I left for Irian Jaya, I had once disregarded all etiquette for missionaries and guest speakers at a missionary conference in Baltimore in the United States and, driven by impatience and frustration, had simply stepped forward and said publicly that the only reason I couldn't go out on the mission field was because there were no resources.

I was sharply reprimanded by the secretary of our missionary society for this inappropriate behavior. I will never forget the words with which he ended his scolding: "The more you said, the more embarrassed I was." That was rather dubious encouragement for a candidate, because I hadn't even told him everything.

Immediately after the event, an obviously well-off lady approached me.

"If I had a million dollars, I would put it at your disposal," she said kindly.

"Dear lady," I replied, "if you want to wait until you have a million dollars, you may never be able to give anything to the mission."

Within a week, the lady sent a check for five hundred dollars. I didn't know at the time that she had long been one of the generous donors who had already given a lot to the mission. She had learned to give, and she practiced this privilege of giving with great faithfulness.

We didn't talk much about these things with the Dani. They were so terribly poor; yet they gave what little they had with joyful hearts. Sometimes it was shameful and amusing at the same time.

In Witiny, a village just outside Mamit, a church service had just finished. Some people had already gotten up to leave, while I remained seated to wait for the men who would accompany me back and who were still busy saying goodbye. Off to the side, I saw a man speaking with the elders. His attitude was friendly but firm. Then he told a small boy to bring a pig that was tied to a nearby tree. The man took it in his arms and came towards me.

"Men . . . ; Kanggipaga . . ." He was obviously searching for the right words. Looking around, he asked one of the elders: "You tell him!" The elder gladly complied with this request: "The man wants you to keep this pig." I was about to say that I wasn't interested in buying a pig when he continued: "He wants to give it to you. Because you helped him to live forever he wants to give you something out of gratitude." "But I didn't give him eternal life," I hastened to assure him.

"But if you hadn't come, I would have died in my sins," the man now said. "Please, accept it!"

As I didn't want to hurt him, I accepted his generous gift. In earlier times, men often killed each other when they fought over a pig. Now a pig was simply given away!

"When he comes to the garden of our heavenly Father, he can't take it with him anyway," explained the elder.

"Well, what do you think? Don't you think I'd like to go there too?" I replied.

General laughter followed. I thanked the man profusely and made my way home. In our company was also a contentedly grunting piglet.

But the whole thing soon got out of hand. I could no longer go anywhere without people offering me their gifts after the service: mainly pigs, later also chickens. Some gave out of gratitude, others to be seen by people. Still others hoped for a useful reward.

I therefore decided not to accept any further tokens of friendship. So as not to offend anyone, I showed my appreciation for their gifts, but at the same time asked them to keep the animals in their home for me. "I'll get it when I need it," I said, not mentioning that I probably wouldn't need it anytime soon.

But even with that statement, I had to be careful. One day a man came running up to me all excited—completely out of breath from the exertion.

"Kanggipaga, can you remember the pig I gave you? Just think, it had ten babies!"

Flying Saucer was so poor that he didn't even own a pig. I knew of his sincerity when one day he came to my house with a whole net full of fresh cucumbers.

"Kanggipaga," he said as deliberately as ever, "my friend Kanggipaga, you have given me eternal life."

I had become so accustomed to this form of expression that I no longer corrected it.

"Kanggipaga, because you've given me so much, I want to give you something too." He carefully placed cucumber after cucumber on the grass. It was almost like a ritual. The gratitude that shone from his eyes far exceeded the value of the cucumbers. I was deeply moved by this overriding generosity.

"But I want to give you something too," I said.

The man looked horrified: "No, no, this is a gift. You've already given me so much. You are my friend."

"Precisely because we're friends, I want to give you something too," I insisted. I ran into the kitchen where I picked up a large packet of salt. The people here were crazy about this salt. In the past, they had only known a dirty substance that had a slightly salty taste. And even that wasn't easy to come by.

Flying Saucer didn't want to get involved in a discussion. He politely thanked me for my gift and left, but the real joy had disappeared from his eyes.

He came back the next day. From my study, I saw him walking stealthily towards the house, and I wondered what he was up to. When he came to the kitchen door, he looked around, then nimbly opened his net and dumped a new load of cucumbers on the floor. Then he ran away as fast as he could. Deep satisfaction was written all over his face. At last he had managed to outwit his friend and deliver a real gift!

FROM SAVAGE TO STUDENT

IN JUNE 1966 we returned from our first furlough. It came somewhat as a disappointment that Field Conference had re-allocated us to Karubaga. So many memories and friends' lives were linked with Mamit. Karubaga was so different. With its longer and better airstrip, small mission hospital, and Bible school, it was not only bigger, but also more impersonal.

But the pattern laid down in the second chapter of Acts held true here as well. The Spirit of God had not only swept through Mamit and Kanggyme, but through Karubaga also.

Luke, the beloved physician, had once written, "The Lord added to the church daily such as should be saved" (Act 2:47). That was the situation in the entire Swart Valley. We now faced the next step in the development of the church: providing trained leadership to support the local assemblies.

In June of the previous year, "Sekolah Alkitab Maranatha," the Maranatha Bible School, had opened its doors in Karubaga. It soon became known as "SAM." Each of the three Swart stations was allowed to send eight or nine students to SAM. Ultimately, the school had an enrolment of ninety male and sixty-five female students.

Entrance requirements were kept as simple as possible: regeneration, a good testimony in the community, proven leadership ability, the ability to read and write.

Of the three first Mamit elders, only Tuwanonuwa fulfilled the requirements. Andugumanggen and Kabutna failed on the fourth point.

The building of the school and facilities was a powerful demonstration of Christian unity, as former enemies worked side-by-side to build living quarters and classrooms for their spiritual leaders-to-be.

After performing general station duties for one year, much like we had done in Mamit, Ruth and I were asked to join the SAM staff. Once again, we found ourselves working together with John and Helen Dekker, formerly from Kanggyme. Through the students we maintained contact with our old stations.

It remains to be seen who learned the most—students or staff. One of my earlier students was Wengguninik. Wengguninik was a spirited little man. War experiences had left him with only one eye.

Our first acquaintance goes back to the early days in Kanggyme. It all came about as a result of my inadequate knowledge of the language. I had asked ten men to get poles from the forest for building purposes. I thought we had agreed that for every forty pieces of wood, each man would receive a steel axe—a prized possession among the stone age Danis. At the end of the day, some hundred men turned up, each one carrying one pole and demanding a steel axe as payment. To me it was outrageous. I didn't even have that many axes in stock. It seemed to me the men were trying me out. Their ringleader was a spirited little man with one eye.

At first he used gentle persuasion. Then he began to put on the pressure, demanding that I hand out the axes immediately. When I wouldn't budge, he became angry and nasty. Gradually he began to lose control over himself. I had seen such scenes before, but only as an onlooker. The situation was becoming critical. The little fellow started running back and forth and jumping up and down. The murmurings of his compatriots grew louder and louder, driving him to greater frenzy. Menacingly, he began to swing his stone axe in front of me. His behaviour was an open invitation to evil spirits, who would take possession of the man as they had always done during the wild dances prior to tribal battles. I knew that if they would take over now, we would all be in serious trouble.

Deliverance came in quite an unexpected way. Ruth was in our hut with Priscilla and John Mark, who was then only a few weeks old. Alarmed by the commotion outside, she appeared in the doorway to see what was going on. Ruth had always been terrified of spiders and other kinds of tiny insects, but now she found the courage to take a stand against a hundred raging Dani men. As white as a sheet and trembling, she left the little house, came over to me, and put her arm around my waist.

Instant confusion resulted. What was this? If she had come storming out of the house brandishing a burning stick or hurling rocks to chase away my antagonists, they would have understood and accepted the challenge. But—why this? What was behind this mysterious behaviour?

The baffled men, who had already witnessed some very strange and inexplicable things with these missionaries, became apprehensive. What followed was as inexplicable to me as my wife's act had been to the angry Danis. The ringleader began to lose support and quietened down himself. Then, one after the other, my assailants withdrew. It was beautiful. A few minutes later, they had all disappeared.

The spirited little one-eyed warrior, of course, was Wengguninik. A number of years after this clash, he graduated from Bible school. Presently, he is in charge of the youth work in the Kanggyme district.

NO BIBLES, PLEASE!

SITTING AT my crudely fashioned desk in one of the SAM classrooms, I looked at my students. I loved teaching these men. What they lacked in elementary knowledge, they made up for in keenness and dedication. We were waiting for the last students to enter.

"What happened to them?" I asked jokingly. "Did they get lost on the way over from chapel?" The chapel, where all students gathered every morning before classes, was about a hundred yards away.

"Perhaps they went home to sleep a little more," someone suggested. The men loved joking. "Sleep?" I responded in mock indignation. "Should a SAM student sleep away his time? Do you think God ever sleeps?" One student took me up on the question.

With an expression of quiet delight on his face, he gently said, "Why should God sleep? It is always light in His presence."

The men loved bantering like that, but sometimes they could all of a sudden turn quite seriously. The remark about God's glory and light led to another question.

"Have you ever met Jesus personally whilst He was still on earth?" someone wanted to know. My denial was reason for some surprise. Now the questions were really coming.

"What about your father? Did he know Jesus before he ascended?"

Once again I had to disappoint my eager listeners.

How could they know? They had no idea about time or distances. Kanggyme and Mamit were *"ndaanda"* or far away from Karubaga, though within walking distance in the same valley. Israel might be just around the corner from the Netherlands. Even the sun was considered to be near. How else would it be possible to feel its heat? When once I, very excitedly, told my students that a man had actually landed on the moon, they were not at all impressed.

"Oké," they said. "When are they going to the sun?" After all, now they were enlightened and knew that planes of the Mission Aviation Fellowship were not evil spirits but manmade machines. You want to go to the sun? Just hop on board and keep flying!

Their notion of time was equally inadequate. Until missionaries came hours, days, weeks and months were unknown. Something in the future might be one or two months away and if it was further away than that, who would care?

So, I took a piece of chalk and started drawing stick-figures on the blackboard to make clear how long ago it was that Jesus walked on earth. Some two thousand years. Obviously that was quite meaningless to my audience. I might as well have said two hundred or twenty thousand years. But I would make things clear to them. Two thousand years or, approximately, some fifty generations. Fifty stick-figures. It would take some time but then, at last, they would understand. The more figures I drew the louder the noise behind me became. When I turned around I saw a sea of exuberantly laughing faces.

"Ai, Kanggypaga," someone called out. You are always trying to fool us. "Everybody knows that people have not existed that long. It is not that long ago since the first humans crawled out of a little hole in the earth." (Another version had it that people had "always" existed).

It took some effort to convince the class that this time I was not joking. When, at last, this became clear, it became absolutely silent in the class There was a strange atmosphere. Something I had not encountered before. A kind of dejection.

Finally, there was a response. The words uttered by one of the students represented undoubtedly the thoughts of them all. They were without any reproach, but at the same time heart-rending and unforgettable, "Why, then, did you wait so long before you came to us with the Good News?"

Anyone willing to answer that question?

We returned to the order of the day, unaware that this profound question would have its effect far across the borders of Dani-land.

When everyone had arrived, I announced that we were going to have a test. Instantaneously, the classroom was a hive of activity. Some started sharpening their pencils as if their lives depended on it. Others quickly left their desks to sit down on the floor, their legs crossed after native fashion. Sitting at a desk like the missionary teacher during lectures was one thing; but to stay in such an uncomfortable and unnatural position whilst concentrating on a difficult test paper was quite another.

Tests were difficult, and they never failed to hold the students in awe. In the beginning they gave rise to a lot of confusion. In our teaching we always stressed the necessity of being helpful and considerate towards others. But when exam time came around, we would change our attitudes mercilessly and without explanation. "You may not help each other," I would warn sternly. "Anyone who does will have to hand in his paper and go outside." To be sent out of class was a terrible disgrace to men who were very much aware of the privilege of being representatives of their home churches.

Our behaviour was even more disconcerting to the students when it came to the use of Scriptures. We continually encouraged them to read and study the Bible, pointing out that it could be a source of comfort and wisdom in times of distress. Surely an exam period was such a time of distress! But what did I say? "No Gospels or other portions of Scripture may be used during the exam." The students were shocked by my inconsistency.

We tried to maintain strict examination rules but somehow failed to make ourselves understood. It was asking for casualties.

Olomban was a loyal and promising elder from Kanggyme. He was a keen student. During one exam, my mouth almost dropped open in unbelief, when I saw this honest, intelligent man casually reaching for one of his Gospel booklets. Without the slightest effort to be secretive, he began leafing through the book.

"Olomban, what are you doing?" I gasped.

He gave me a look of innocent helplessness. "I just can't remember the correct answer to this question. I know it, but it just won't come to mind." He smiled. "I know it's in this book. I know it for certain. I just read it the other day." I finally got the message. We would have to present our exams in a different way. How could we ever have thought of disallowing the use of Scriptures when the whole of our teaching programme was directed at encouraging it? Sometimes the Danis could be hard to refute!

MISSING, BELIEVED KILLED

There were no classes in the afternoon except English, which I did not teach. I went to my study and sat down, savouring the prospect of an undisturbed afternoon to prepare teaching materials.

A simple Dani commentary on the book of Acts had already been completed, and so had several booklets on the life of Christ. I loved this kind of work. In spite of the hardships, I never ceased to be amazed at the privilege of being in full-time missionary service. Contentedly, I looked around my study, running my eyes along the shelves of books. We had discarded the greater part of our library before coming to the field. I loved the few books that were left all the more. I loved my little study. The temperature in the room was a comfortable twenty-seven degrees Centigrade. The calendar indicated September 26, 1968.

The sound of a motorbike pulling up to a halt in front of the house aroused me from my reveries. I frowned. These hateful interruptions! Dave Martin, a Canadian colleague, came bursting up the stairs and into my study. His face was pale, his voice tense. His words were to mark the end of my preparations for many days to come.

"Stan and Phil are missing; believed killed!" he gasped and helplessly sat down on the wooden floor.

Stan Dale and Philip Masters were also missionaries with RBMU. Stan was Australian and Phil American. They were stationed in the Eastern Highlands, at Ninia and Koruppun respectively.

The mission station of Ninia was opened in March 1962; Koruppun not until January 1964. The Yali and Kimyal tribes living in that region had responded very differently to the Gospel than the Danis of the Swart Valley.

On September 19, Stan and Phil had left Koruppun together, planning to check the language border between the two stations, preach the Gospel in the villages en route and look for a possible location for an airstrip. Three Dani carriers from Karubaga and one man from Ninia accompanied them. This was not the first missionary journey through that area. A few years earlier, Stan and co-worker, Bruno de Leeuw, had trekked through parts of the same valley. They didn't encounter any particular difficulties.

Dave Martin sat on the floor in my study. He had received a radio call from Angguruk at 1:15 that afternoon. Two of the Karubaga men accompanying Stan and Phil, Ndenggeniyak and Nigitanggen, had arrived at that station, reporting that Stan and Phil had been attacked and killed.

I was not overly concerned by what Dave told me. Many of us had been threatened at one time or another. News from the grapevine was not always reliable. There were many questions and obviously, Dave did not have sufficient information to supply the answers.

"Good thing Frank is here," I said. "Let's see what he has to suggest."

Frank Clarke, stationed at Mamit, happened to be in Karubaga for a few days. He was our field superintendent for that year and therefore was the man to decide what action needed to be taken. Wisely, Frank didn't take any chances. He immediately contacted MAF (Mission Aviation Fellowship), requesting a plane to investigate the place where the killings were reported to have occurred. On the spur of the moment I decided to join him. "If I were in Stan or Phil's place, I'm sure Ruth would appreciate it if someone volunteered to find out what had happened," I told myself. She fully agreed.

Not long after that, Frank and I were airborne. Paul Pontier, nicknamed Pablo because he had done a stint in Central America, flew us in to Angguruk to pick up Ndenggeniyak and Nigitanggen. They proved excellent guides. With amazing accuracy, they pinpointed the various places they

MISSING, BELIEVED KILLED 179

Stan Dale and family

Phil Masters and family

had trekked through the previous days. Winding our way through the mountains in our little Cessna, we tried to pick up any possible clues as to the whereabouts of Phil and Stan. When we came close to the area we wanted to survey most, we had to call off our search. Heavy clouds had rolled into the valley, hiding it from view.

Pablo flew us to his home base of Wamena, in the Baliem Valley. Nothing else could be done that day.

The situation now seemed more serious than I had initially thought. We questioned the two Danis extensively, but could not arrive at any definite conclusions.

"They shot our fathers," both men stated emphatically.

"Did you see that they were dead?"

"We saw how they shot them."

"Perhaps they were only injured?"

'They shot them with many arrows."

We were pushing for more answers than the fellows, who had barely managed to escape themselves, could honestly provide. The gnawing uncertainty remained.

At 5:50 PM the transmitter-receiver at Wamena crackled into life. "Wamena, Wamena-Angguruk over."

Paul jumped towards the set.

"Angguruk-Wamena, go ahead, over."

"Roger, Paul. Jimo, a carrier from Ninia who accompanied Stan and Phil, has just turned up here. He confirms that Stan and Phil were attacked and are dead. Over."

"Did he actually see they were dead? Over."

"Negative; he started running at the same time as the Karubaga fellows. But he says they are dead. Over."

That was the end of the conversation. It was good to know that Jimo had escaped to safety. But what about Stan and Phil? Were they really killed or merely injured? And if injured, how badly?

Where were they? Could they have been captured alive? And what about the third Karubaga man, Ndenggen? We had not heard a word about him. We kept turning the questions over and over in our minds.

As we were sitting around the meal Ruthie Pontier had prepared for us, suddenly, unexpectedly, the radio sprang to life again. It was a highly unusual time of day for radio traffic. A male voice became audible.

"Phil!" all four of us shouted in chorus.

The voice transmitted a few brief sentences, but static garbled them up beyond understanding—Phil's message was lost.

Immediately Paul acknowledged through the transmitter that we were listening. No answer. He asked for the message to be repeated, changed channels, tried a blind transmission.[1] It was all to no avail. No matter what we tried, there was no further communication. But there was hope!

We went to bed early, but no one slept much that night.

The beautiful stillness of the morning stood in strange contrast to our own feelings. We were anxious to get going. Our hearts were filled with questions, doubts, hopes, and fears, yet, strangely, we could not help but praise God together for His beautiful creation. The sun had barely risen above the horizon. A lone bird tentatively began its morning song.

Paul fired the Cessna engine. The sound of the engine shattered the silence of the morning. We rolled towards the take-off area, requesting clearance.

The plane rushed forward full throttle, as if it knew that an urgent task lay ahead. The earth fell away.

Tiny tufts of silvery blue smoke drifted upwards from the grass roofs of the huts beneath us: the natives were cooking their breakfast of sweet potatoes. A little brown figure could be seen making its way to a nearby spring.

The dark brown water of the Baliem River flowed sluggishly beneath us, like a thick, sickeningly sweet chocolate paste. We gained altitude and the chilly morning air penetrated the cabin. I shivered.

We decided to call at Ninia first. Perhaps our missing colleagues had arrived there in the night or early morning. When the sun-drenched station came into view, it seemed strangely quiet. There wasn't a living being on the airstrip. No cheering wreath of smoke rose from the chimney

---

1   That is, a frequency with no guarantee of reception.

of the Dales' house. There was no one in their yard. The whole place was deserted. It didn't look good.

Despite the "hard labour" of missionaries and Danis, the Ninia airstrip was horrible. When a plane landed at the bottom of the strip, it could not be seen from the top. Its construction had taken almost a year, much longer than any of the strips in the Swart. The locals had been hesitant to dig around in the soil where the spirits were supposed to be living.

We breathed a prayer as Pablo made his final approach. "The engine dropped," the ground surged up to us. Touchdown. Being jolted and bounced up and down as we taxied up the bumpy airstrip was like an answer to prayer. We had landed safely. Alerted by the noise of our aircraft, Luliap came running. He was one of Stan's trusted men.

"My father has not arrived yet," he said hastily. "He is still out on the trail with Piliput." This was the Jali way of saying Philip. Luliap, who assumed that we were merely paying a visit, had not heard the latest news. When we told him, he was stunned. "Oh, my father," he said. "What will they have done to my father?"

Leaving Ninia, we flew once more to the area where the attack was supposed to have occurred. It was of no use. The spot was hidden in a deep gorge with densely wooded sides. In order to gain access to the area, Frank decided to order a helicopter from Papua New Guinea—the nearest place where there was one stationed. On we flew, to Koruppun, where Pat Dale and Phyliss Masters were anxiously awaiting further news about their husbands.

Extensive use of their radio had drained its battery. They had been cut off from the outside world for several hours. That day Pat was shuttled to Ninia and Phyliss to Karubaga to await further developments there.

"I keep hoping, Jacques," Phyliss said before she boarded the plane. She smiled courageously.

The helicopter was supposed to land in Ninia that afternoon. Frank and I went there to wait for its arrival. When it finally touched down, the day was too far gone for us to undertake anything. Thick clouds had rolled into the gorge, making any landing there impossible. If the weather cooperated, the next morning would be the earliest opportunity for getting a closer look at the area where Phil and Stan had last been seen. The radio remained silent that evening. As tension increased, hope diminished. There was no doubt now: something was seriously wrong.

We turned in early that night again. Every possible course of action had been mulled over, every option discussed. We could only hope and pray that the morning would come quickly.

I was lying on my air mattress, unable to sleep. My thoughts turned to Ruth and the children, back in Karubaga. How would they cope with the tension and uncertainty?

That was the worst thing, the uncertainty. We did not know where Stan and Phil were. We didn't even know whether they were alive or dead. If only there were some signs, something to renew our hope—or else, if need be, to put to an end any false hopes. If only we knew.

In the darkness of the Ninia night, I began to reflect on my own position. From the moment Dave Martin had bolted into my study the previous afternoon, an eerie reality had begun to take shape in the back of my mind. Now it stared me straight in the face: *"This time tomorrow, you may be dead yourself."*

If Phil and Stan had been killed, their murderers would be delirious. Even the most antagonistic of tribes had always stood in awe of the mysterious white man and his apparent supernatural powers. The deaths of Phil and Stan vould have changed that. Any fear the Jalis may have had for the white man would have been drowned in the excitement of the killing. Having drawn white men's blood, the savage Jali warriors would be thirsty for more. Hardly the best of the circumstances for paying them a visit by helicopter!

I prayed silently. *"Lord Jesus, I commit my life into Your hands. Thank you that everything is alright between you and me."* I prayed for Ruth and our children.

I woke up when Frank started stirring the next morning. It was five o'clock. I had not slept so peacefully for a long time. We had barely finished our breakfast of cold rice when Ninia was already buzzing with activity. Bob Hamilton was checking out his chopper. Pablo flew in a number of Indonesian military men from Wamena. Weather conditions looked perfect:

a bright blue sky with only a few patches of white cloud. This was the day. Tension rose. If there had been an opportunity, I would have backed out. But there was no turning back.

Frank and one military man lifted off at 6:05 AM. Bob dropped them in the general area of the alleged attack. He was back in about 20 minutes, to pick up two more soldiers. When he came back for the third time, it was my turn.

"Hurry up," Bob shouted as I boarded the chopper. "The natives are pouring in from all sides."

My heart sank. An army corporal jumped in next to me, handing me a gun. I had never flown in a helicopter before. We were off.

Bob's words echoed in my ears. *"They're pouring in from all sides."* What were we trying to do anyway—half a dozen men against a horde of blood-thirsty, intoxicated warriors? We didn't stand a chance! Was this the end? I tried to pray, but couldn't. I was too tense. "Jesus, oh Jesus," I whispered. He was right there. A loving, encouraging, and understanding Person, radiant with light and peace. His presence was so real it took me by surprise. "If I stretch out my hand, I can touch His arm," I thought. It was an overwhelming experience.

We landed on a flat piece of ground near a riverbed. High mountain peaks towered up above us on all sides. The ridges were lined with warriors. We could hear their voices. Each one was armed to the teeth.

"They won't come," Corporal Sadely assured me. "Just before we landed, my colleague fired a volley through the valley. The echo in these mountains was like thunder." He smiled. "They won't come. They're afraid." Keeping my thoughts to myself, I wondered just how long the angry warriors would remain afraid.

Frank and the other military men were not there. Bob had dropped them closer to the place where things were supposed to have happened. So there I stood, with Lilly Sadely, an Indonesian man I had never set eyes on before. There wasn't much to say. Besides, we had difficulty speaking each other's language. We kept our eyes glued to the ridges.

High above us the weather was changing. More and more clouds began to fill the still bright blue sky. Swirled about by the wind, they slowly began to build up around the mountain peaks, threatening to close off our only exit. Above the peaks, Pablo flew a lonely vigilance, keeping an eye on the people below him and above us. I longed for the safe shelter of his tiny cabin. It seemed as distant as the remotest star.

I breathed a sigh of relief when suddenly I heard the familiar *tak-etak-tak* of the returning chopper. Hurriedly, we boarded. A few minutes later we landed at Ninia. I was glad we would not be spending a night in that fearful valley. Hamilton rushed off to pick up Frank and the others before the gap closed. They barely made it.

There was more news than some of us had anticipated. Frank had brought back the kind of evidence which we had hoped would not be there. His report was sober.

"After landing in a dry riverbed, a fifteen minute walk brought us right to the site. There was clothing and camping gear scattered around. Judging from the broken-off arrows lying around, I'd estimate that Stan received seventy-five to one hundred arrows and Phil somewhat less. Their clothing was bristling with arrows. It is certain beyond doubt, that Stan and Phil have been killed. We were not able to find the bodies. There was evidence that they were mutilated and cut up before being carried off to the village."

There was one piece of material evidence to support Frank's conclusions. It was small, but devastatingly sure. He opened his hand: in his palm lay a small piece of jawbone holding a tooth with a filling. Stone Age tribespeople do not have fillings.

Frank also brought back some arrowheads. When I held them, my hands were bloody. "I'm sorry fellows," I said softly. Our mission had abruptly come to an end.

For the moment there was nothing else we could do. Just before evening fell, I flew back to Karubaga. Phyliss had moved into our guest room. The last time she had stayed with us had been on April 9, when our two families had celebrated Phil's thirty-seventh birthday together. It had been his last. Now he was gone.[1]

---

1 Stan and Phil were killed by the Jalis in the Seng Valley of the Eastern Highlands of Irian Jaya.

I broke the final and unalterable truth to Phyliss. Her strength of character enabled her to receive the news with courage and quiet dignity. She gently told her children, who had been flown in from the boarding school on the coast. Even as young children, they reacted with composure. Curtis, Phil's oldest son, simply remarked: "Why did they kill my father? He never harmed anybody." It was an affectionate understatement about a man who had laid down his life for Christ's sake.

On March 30, 1969, Timothy Philip Masters was born, just over six months after the death of his father on September 25, 1968. Phyliss Masters later forgave her husband's murderers and witnessed many Yali converts to Christ.[1]

Phyliss Masters and tiny Timothy Philip

The fourth carrier who had accompanied Phil and Stan, a Dani named Ndenggen, was never heard from again. Apparently, he escaped into the forest only to die of hunger, cold, and exhaustion as he tried to cross the high mountain passes in order to reach Karubaga. We honoured his memory in a special service. In a very real sense, Ndenggen was the first martyr of the Dani church.

---

1 The life stories of the two murdered missionaries Phil Masters and Stan Dale can be read in: *Lords of the Earth* by Don Richardson.

MBURUMBURU GOES HOME

AROUND THAT time, word reached us from Mamit that Mburumburu had died. The way in which it happened befitted the gentle old man. He had never been an outstanding spiritual leader, yet his unswerving loyalty and devotion to his Saviour made him a unique and exemplary Christian. Mburumburu walked with God. He talked with God as with a friend, and God talked with him. The way in which he went home proved that.

He was quite frail when I last saw him. He had never been a robust fellow, but now, his slender body seemed to be a mere shadow. His frame was bent forward. His cheeks were hollow, his voice raspy. Only the spirit within him remained fresh and strong and free.

Eerariyakkwe, his wife, who was at least as old, came all the way from Mamit to tell us about Mburumburu's last hours. She looked a bit like a witch with her bent-over body, bony fingers, and single yellow tooth protruding from her gums. But her spirit was pure like that of her husband. The story that fell from her cracked lips was as sweet as it was simple.

"Kanggypaga, your friend Mburumburu has gone home," she began. Even though this was an unusual way of saying that someone had died, I knew immediately what she meant.

"One day Mburumburu came home," she began "He was tired."

"Eerariyakkwe," he croaked. "I would like you to cook some leaves of the sweet potato for me. After you cook them, I will eat them." He spoke like a typical Dani, formulating short sentences and in each new sentence referring to the previous one. "After I eat them, I will go to the yard of my heavenly Father."

"*Ai,* my husband," Eerariyakkwe replied. That was typical, too. It was one of those Dani exclamations that could mean everything and nothing.

"*Ai,* my husband," she repeated. "I will cook the leaves quickly for you. After I cook them quickly, you will eat them."

Mburumburu watched his wife produce the leaves from a net bag which dangled on a peg in their hut. Lifelong experience in the cumbersome art of steam cooking made it appear simple. It was not long before Eerariyakkwe removed the hot stones with a forked stick and presented the leaves to her husband.

Mburumburu and Eerariyakkwe

"I will eat," he announced customarily, before stuffing the steaming, succulent leaves into his mouth.

After Mburumburu had had his fill, Eerariyakkwe ate. When she was finished, Mburumburu shifted backward and leaned his body against the rough wooden wall of their hut. He uttered a sigh of contentment and closed his eyes. He didn't fall asleep though. Just as he had said he would, he quietly passed into the presence of his Lord. He had arrived in the yard of his Father. Mburumburu was home.

When she had finished relating her story, looking at her peaceful features, I asked Eerariyakkwe, "Why aren't you sad?" My question seemed to surprise her.

"Why should I be? Soon I'll be going there myself."

At that moment I felt like crying myself—for pure joy! This was the fruit of our labour! This was the power of the Gospel! Previously, thousands of Danis had died, fearful and without hope. Survivors had literally run around in circles, screaming and lamenting. And that was not all. Uncertain about the intentions of the deceased, people would cut off parts of their ears with sharp strips of bamboo, or chop fingers off with stone axes (without anesthetic), to be thrown into the funeral pyre as a sacrifice to the departed spirit.

If Mburumburu had been the only one, it would have been worth every effort, but now there were thousands ready to go to their Father's yard, because their names are written in the Book of Life.

190   THE SECRET OF NABELAN KABELAN

For each deceased relative, a finger was chopped off

END OF AN ERA

I T IS June 16, 1974. We are standing on the airstrip of Karubaga. After thirteen years of labour and love shared with the Dani tribespeople, our time is up.

Revolutionary changes had swept across the Swart Valley in the course of those thirteen years. We had come to a heathen tribe, living in the stone age and totally ignorant of God and His Word. Now the majority of Danis in the Swart were born-again Christians. Seventy-three local churches had been established, each with its own indigenous leadership. Since the day SAM opened its doors, one hundred seventeen students had graduated. The young churches were vigorous and healthy. Each congregation had at least one missionary couple in other parts of Irian Jaya, among people of different cultures and languages. Despite extreme poverty, each couple was supported by its home church. Obviously, foreign missionaries would still be needed for a long time to come, but still an era was coming to a close. Our time, in any case, was up; a different task lay ahead.

The twin-engine Aero Commander has just landed. Busy hands are unloading its cargo. The moment of truth has come. Our few belongings have already been placed on board. We came with little and we will leave with little—though we trust we are both leaving behind and taking with us a rich spiritual heritage. Missionary colleagues stand around the plane.

Someone cracks a joke. Saying goodbye is part of the missionary life; but that does not make it any easier.

Someone wants to take a photograph. The kids of the village school sing a farewell song. The wind picks up their thin voices and carries them away across the valley. I look at the black faces lining the strip. No one speaks. A few men are crying unashamedly. Jan, the beloved SAM teacher, is not here. He was afraid he would break down. I see old Leenggwa. *"This will be the last time on earth,"* I think.

Glen Laird, the pilot, asks us to get on board. As usual, there is a mix-up with the safety-belts. Then the doors slam shut. The Dani station hand gives the "thumbs-up" sign to indicate that the wheel-blocks have been removed and all is clear. The left engine springs to life with a sharp crack. The right one follows. Glen systematically checks the instrument panel. He revs up the engines. A last wave.

We thunder down the airstrip, engines roaring. The nose-wheel loses touch with the ground. Familiar features suddenly sink beneath us, diminishing in size. With a dull thump, the landing gear withdraws itself in its housing.

We have left Irian Jaya.

The plane wings its way out of the familiar valley. Just around the corner lies Kanggyme; over to the left, Mamit.

My mind travels back to one of my last experiences in Mamit, shortly before our first furlough.

With a couple of men, we are sitting around the fire in one of the huts. Tuwanonuwa, Andugumanggen, and Kabutna are there. So is Kimbameryme. Soon he will go to SAM with the first group of students from Mamit. The men are talking in subdued tones. Recalling the past is a beloved past-time among the Danis. The men share their memories like little boys recounting after-school escapades.

"Did you ever want to kill me?" I suddenly ask.

Though we have no secrets from each other, the men envelop themselves in an embarrassed silence. A young fellow tries unsuccessfully to suppress a snicker. He decides to speak.

"Sure," he says, still embarrassed.

"Then why did you never do it?" I persist.

Their amazement is genuine.

"We don't know, really . . ." someone ventures. "We just never got around to doing it."

All along, God has been in charge. It was a Dani custom to murder any stranger entering the tribe. But He did not allow them to put me to death, so that I might be to them a messenger of life. Jesus Christ broke their tradition of killing, offering them instead the secret of *Nabelan Kabelan*.

CONVERSATION WITH JACQUES AND RUTH TEEUWEN

Veronika Trautmann: "While working on this book, I thought a lot about how the first part—your life story or your career—is inextricably linked to the second part—the missionary story. For example, your career aspiration to become a farmer. In the Netherlands, as you say, that was hopeless, but in Irian Jaya you were probably able to utilize some of the things you learned: At least you had a chicken farm there, you introduced different vegetables, etc. Then I also think of the incredibly hard times you had to go through during the Second World War. Without this 'hardening', however, you might not have had the courage to go to such a 'wild' country among warlike people, even if you don't gloss over the fact that you were sometimes afraid. Your character seems to have always been combative and adventurous, it's just that faith has turned you towards a completely different goal, so to speak."

Jacques: "It is true that much of my 'prehistory' may have played a role or even benefited me later, as difficult as it was at first. As far as the war years are concerned, not even Ruth, after forty years of marriage, can fully comprehend—although I have talked about it so often—what tragedies took place back then, how much the whole thing affected me and how deep the despair and senselessness were in which I still found myself years after the war. For me, it is one of God's greatest miracles that my conversion really did free me overnight, so to speak, from the tormenting thoughts of that time, because I know people who are still suffering from them today."

Veronika Trautmann: "When you arrived in Irian Jaya, what were the biggest practical problems following? What was the hardest thing for you to cope with emotionally? As a mother, I also think about the fact that Ruth was expecting her second child at the time, all the circumstances surrounding the subsequent births, dealing with the people there and so on . . ."

Ruth: "One of the biggest problems for me at the beginning was that we could never be alone. There was simply no privacy! As soon as we left our little house, we were immediately surrounded by many people who wanted to touch us and our baby—and they were so dirty! I found this very difficult because many people suffered from the skin disease I have already described, and I knew that my children could get the same thing. For me as a mother, it was really a matter of asking God for help to accept these dirty people and allow them to come into contact with my children.

We had completed a short medical course—not just for us, but also for the people there—and often had to be the doctors for our family ourselves. Otherwise, we could only get medical help if we contacted a doctor via the radio. There were rare illnesses that our children also got. However, during the time we spent with the Dani, we were not seriously ill until one day when our eldest son fell ill with life-threatening diarrhea at the age of one and a half. However, God sent us help. One of the natives offered to walk eight hours over the mountain that very night to get medicine from a doctor. This saved the life of our little John-Mark, and we could not thank God enough for His care.

The most difficult thing for us as a family was that we had to send our children to boarding school. They had to leave us at the age of six and only came home twice a year—during the summer and Christmas vacations. Perhaps Jacques can tell us how God helped us in this difficult situation."

Jacques: "Priscilla left first, then John-Mark a year later, and finally all four of them took off in the plane at the same time—250 km over the jungle, which also involved danger. We were then alone at home, and it felt as if someone had died, it was so quiet and so sad. We sat down and cried together, and I asked God in my distress: 'Lord, why does this have to happen to us?" Then God said in his kindness: 'It happened to me too! I too sent my son into the world, but not to put him in a boarding school so that he could be looked after by Christian house parents, but so that he could be crucified!'

The Word of God tells us that we must be conformed to the image of His Son. Through our personal experience we understood more about the love of our God, but also about the suffering of a Christian."

Ruth: "The two middle sons were born in Irian Jaya, and the fourth child—Stephen—during a home leave in England. John-Mark was born in a hut with a grass roof and a sandy floor. He was delivered on a kitchen table. The midwife only arrived 15 minutes before the birth. She was from Australia and lived not far away. But because there was fighting going on between the villages at the time, no one could communicate with her. At the same time, Jacques had an infection and wasn't feeling well at all. When little John-Mark was born, Jacques couldn't even stand on his feet.

Because it was so dirty everywhere, all attempts to keep the objects clean were in vain—the baby and our older daughter Priscilla developed a skin rash, medically called Impetigo, within a few hours of the little one's birth, which was a hard blow for me. I cried a lot because the Lord had given us this beautiful little baby, but hours later, his skin was already covered in blisters. Nevertheless, I trusted in God that he would prove to be a solid rock and would not let us down.

In the beginning, there were only simple chores. It was enough work to feed the family and keep it clean. Most of our food had come from Australia or the Netherlands, by ship, then by truck, and finally the food was loaded onto small planes, that brought everything to us. But often there were no deliveries for months, so we lacked a lot of things. I first had to learn to bake bread in a wood-fired oven. Later, we were able to train a local boy to help us with the housework so that I could teach in the elementary school and later in the Bible school and be a help to the people."

Veronika Trautmann: "It would be interesting to know whether the churches in your mission area have developed as vibrantly as they did at the beginning. Are you still in contact with the people in Irian Jaya?"

Jacques: "Yes, we still have connections, but you have to imagine that a stamp is very expensive there. That's why we don't write much, but we still hear something from time to time. One of the letters I liked best was from a local man who had become a teacher. He wrote to us in the Netherlands: 'I have never thanked you for being my teacher, but I would like to do so today because I now know how difficult it must have been because I am now a teacher myself.'

The churches are still moving forward. In September, 1993, I received a photo of one of these local boys who had been in my Bible school about twenty-five years ago. At that time he had been almost naked—but in the picture he was shown wearing dark trousers, a white shirt and black tie. He was sitting behind a computer and had translated the Old Testament into his mother tongue.

The situation of the churches today is very good. In our valley—in the Swart Valley—there are no more foreign missionaries, and you could really say that things are developing smoothly there."

Veronika Trautmannn: "You write about new tasks after you left Irian Jaya. How did your life continue after that?"

Jacques: "As clearly as the Lord had given us the call to go to New Guinea, He also clearly showed us that it was time to return. We had offers from America and England to go into the Christian ministry there, but somehow we had no peace about it, and it seemed that the Lord wanted to lead us back to the Netherlands. This seemed illogical to us because our children did not speak Dutch. They didn't have Dutch names either, because we had never thought that we would go back to the Netherlands.

After all, I was in the Netherlands and didn't know what to do at first. About a year later, I attended a conference where I met the leader of an Eastern mission.[1] He came up to me and asked: 'Would you like to work with us behind the Iron Curtain? I couldn't decide immediately and hoped to get clarity at a subsequent conference. There was a woman there who sang Psalm 27:1: 'The Lord is my light and my salvation, of whom shall I be afraid?'—the same verse the Lord had given us when we were on the ship off the coast of New Guinea, and I was really afraid once again, because I was wondering what to do next: Ruth was pregnant at the time, our little daughter Priscilla was only two years old—and we were supposed to join the 'wild ones.' I got the same verse in that situation. Now I had the impression again that God was speaking to me through this verse.

In 1975, I made my first trip behind the Iron Curtain, which gave me new confirmation. In the former GDR (German Democratic Republic), we met a Lutheran pastor who suddenly said to me that I should talk to his mother, who was suffering from leg vein thrombosis. I prayed with her and within eight days she was completely healed. That was the first confirmation.

On the onward journey, there were problems at the border from the GDR to Poland. We were praying again when suddenly someone knocked on the window. The customs officer didn't know what it meant; someone was shouting something. Anyway, he shrugged his shoulders, signed and stamped our papers at once and we were able to drive on. The second confirmation.

After all, we were in Poland, although I didn't know our destination beforehand for security reasons. So I didn't ask where we were going until we were already inland. When I heard the name of the town, I remembered that I had been there once before, during the Hitler Youth training at the end of the Second World War. Among other things, we had been taught there that Christians should be killed because they stood in the way of the progress of national socialism.

Thiry-one years later, we were on our way to this city again. Was it a coincidence that I was there for the first time in the East giving my testimony? The third confirmation.

---

1 Open Doors

We wanted to drive on to the Czech Republic to meet a priest there. But we were warned that it was too dangerous because an informer lived next door and the phone was tapped. So we were advised not to go. Then the doorbell rang and suddenly the priest we had been talking about was standing in the room, even though he couldn't have known we were there.

So the first trip already brought many confirmations, and from then on we always undertook the many trips with great freedom."

Ruth: "For me, Jacques' call to work in Eastern Europe was much more frightening than the call to New Guinea, where we had gone together as a couple. It took me quite a while to accept the fact that God had this plan for us. I was simply more afraid than when we were called to New Guinea. But God allowed me to accept His will. He gave me peace about it and the certainty that he would be with us if this was our path. What Jacques just told me was also a great encouragement to me."

Jacques: "I said that it took a year before I knew what my next assignment was; and because I had always wanted to go to the Eastern states, I later didn't understand why I was unsure for so long. But I realized that it was simply fear. The people on New Guinea were dangerous, they killed you in no time; but I also know a story about a missionary who was caught in the East. He was told to talk now, and because he didn't want to talk, he was told: 'We'll lock you up: no one will know where you are, and if you want to talk later, we won't care. You'll just stay there until you rot.' That really got to me, and I realized that it was the reason why I didn't immediately recognize my future calling."

Veronika Trautmann: "So your original wish to work as a missionary in the Eastern states was fulfilled after all. In hindsight, what do you think of the fact that God first sent you to Irian Jaya before you were able to start your work behind the Iron Curtain?"

Jacques: "Our time in Irian Jaya was like an apprenticeship. We learned there how to be reasonably patient and how to behave in dangerous situations.

I'm now pretty convinced that if I hadn't had this preliminary training, I wouldn't have been able to serve behind the Iron Curtain. Because I needed a lot of patience there, and sometimes it was also dangerous—when we smuggled Bibles and other things—but we learned how to deal with such situations in Irian Jaya."

Ruth: "Our family's missionary story does not end here. Although some of our children have grown up in boarding school, they have learned the essentials: They have recognized the importance of the Christian message and want to carry it out to other countries. Our four children are now all married, and the three older ones are already involved in missionary work. Only the youngest son, Stephen, lives with his family in the Netherlands, the others are in faraway countries—Priscilla in Argentina, Andrew in Albania, John-Mark in England, but of course our greatest joy is that they are all following the path of faith."

Walking Together Press is a non-profit publishing company devoted to supporting grassroots libraries in Africa through global book sales and through providing free library editions.

To read our story, to see our catalog, and to learn more about how you can help us in our mission, visit our website at:

walkingtogether.press